WERE THE WHOLE REALM OF NAT

A Vet's Devotional Memoirs

Norman Page

With illustrations by
Philip Snow

Let the words of my mouth, and the meditation of my heart, be acceptable in thy sight, O LORD, my strength, and my redeemer.

Psalm 19:14

 New Generation Publishing

PREFACE

'Were the Whole Realm of Nature Mine' is a line from the well-known hymn: *'When I Survey the Wondrous Cross'*. It is the author's conviction that the love of God revealed in Creation, as ultimately redeemed and perfected in Christ, will one day glorify its Creator, beyond all that we can now conceive. For it is written, *'Eye hath not seen, nor ear heard, neither have entered into the heart of man, the things which God hath prepared for them that love him.'* No offering, even the whole of Creation, would have been enough to redeem even one of us. But at Calvary, none other than the Creator himself was offered. *'Love so amazing, so divine, demands my soul, my life, my all!'*

The 52 illustrated memoirs recorded here, sketch the author's journey from a small boy on a farm, through to his life as a veterinary surgeon in his beloved rural England. They take us from the 'Paradise-Lost' of early childhood, to an experience of becoming *'as a little child'* again. Thus, it may safely be said, this is a book for *'children'* of all ages!

And can it be, that there's provision-enough for every soul of man to be restored, along with the rest of Creation? How wonderful to discover that there is, indeed, a well of salvation, springing-up into everlasting life. A place where we need never thirst again, and where God shall wipe away all tears from our eyes.

Herein then, is a message of divine love, which, as we look out on a world of confusion and doubt, rebellion and conflict, sorrow and suffering, is as urgent now as ever. For as long as the earth remains, the good seed of God's eternal word must be sown.

The Scripture quotations are all from the Authorized King James Version of the Bible (AKJV). Although the language is 'old fashioned', it retains its cutting-edge. Born of the fires of the sixteenth century Reformation martyrs, it became the cultural bedrock of the English-speaking world.

It is the author's prayer that these personal reflections will, in the good and pleasant company of *'the Interpreter'*, the Holy Spirit, bring the light of Christ to all who engage with them.

Norman Page, Spring 2017

God, who at sundry times and in divers manners spake in time past unto the fathers by the prophets, hath in these last days spoken unto us by his Son, whom he hath appointed heir of all things, by whom also he made the worlds; who being the brightness of his glory, and the express image of his person, and upholding all things by the word of his power, when he had by himself purged our sins, sat down on the right hand of the Majesty on high.

Hebrews 1:1-3

Acknowledgements

The author wishes to thank all who provided such kind help and encouragement, in what has been a joyful expression of praise to God at the end of his working life. Many of the photographs are from his everyday travels in Shropshire, some even from his own garden. Those supplied by friends are acknowledged by footnote, and where authentic original photographs could not be obtained, wildlife artist Philip Snow came alongside, fully identifying with the book's purpose. Valued preliminary work on publication was provided by Tim Pagden; and hymn copyright issues clarified by Liz Millard, of the Methodist Church Connexional Team. Finally, thanks are due to the team at New Generation Publishing, for their help in presenting the manuscript to the world at large.

THE TWO GREAT BOOKS

Thy word is a lamp unto my feet, and a light unto my path

Psalm 119:105

But ask now the beasts, and they shall teach thee; and the fowls of the air, and they shall tell thee: or speak to the earth, and it shall teach thee: and the fishes of the sea shall declare unto thee. Who knoweth not in all these that the hand of the LORD hath wrought this? In whose hand is the soul of every living thing, and the breath of all mankind.

Job 12:7–10

...though he were a Son, yet learned he obedience by the things which he suffered; and being made perfect, he became the author of eternal salvation unto all them that obey him.

Hebrews 5:8-9

TITLE HYMN

When I survey the wondrous cross
On which the Prince of Glory died,
My richest gain I count but loss,
And pour contempt on all my pride.

Forbid it, Lord, that I should boast,
Save in the death of Christ my God!
All the vain things that charm me most,
I sacrifice them to His blood.

See from His head, His hands, His feet,
Sorrow and love flow mingled down!
Did e'er such love and sorrow meet,
Or thorns compose so rich a crown?

Were the whole realm of nature mine,
That were an offering far too small;
Love so amazing, so divine,
Demands my soul, my life, my all.

Isaac Watts, 1674-1748

Now is the judgment of this world: now shall the prince of this world be cast out. And I, if I be lifted up from the earth, will draw all men unto me. This he said, signifying what death he should die.

John 12:31-33.

THE PROPHET ISAIAH: CHAPTER 53

*Who hath believed our report? and to whom is the arm of the L*ORD *revealed? For he shall grow up before him as a tender plant, and as a root out of a dry ground: he hath no form nor comeliness; and when we shall see him, there is no beauty that we should desire him. He is despised and rejected of men; a man of sorrows, and acquainted with grief: and we hid as it were our faces from him; he was despised, and we esteemed him not. Surely he hath borne our griefs, and carried our sorrows: yet we did esteem him stricken, smitten of God, and afflicted. But he was wounded for our transgressions, he was bruised for our iniquities: the chastisement of our peace was upon him; and with his stripes we are healed. All we like sheep have gone astray; we have turned every one to his own way; and the L*ORD *hath laid on him the iniquity of us all. He was oppressed, and he was afflicted, yet he opened not his mouth: he is brought as a lamb to the slaughter, and as a sheep before her shearers is dumb, so he openeth not his mouth. He was taken from prison and from judgment: and who shall declare his generation? for he was cut off out of the land of the living: for the transgression of my people was he stricken. And he made his grave with the wicked, and with the rich in his death; because he had done no violence, neither was any deceit in his mouth. Yet it pleased the L*ORD *to bruise him; he hath put him to grief: when thou shalt make his soul an offering for sin, he shall see his seed, he shall prolong his days, and the pleasure of the L*ORD *shall prosper in his hand. He shall see of the travail of his soul, and shall be satisfied: by his knowledge shall my righteous servant justify many; for he shall bear their iniquities. Therefore will I divide him a portion with the great, and he shall divide the spoil with the strong; because he hath poured out his soul unto death: and he was numbered with the transgressors; and he bare the sin of many, and made intercession for the transgressors.*

Written c. 700 years BC

CONTENTS

EPILOGUE:

Jesus answered and said unto her, Whosoever drinketh of this water shall thirst again: but whosoever drinketh of the water that I shall give him shall never thirst; but the water that I shall give him shall be in him a well of water springing up into everlasting life.

John 4:13-14

1

EARLIEST MEMORIES

Some of my most vivid early memories are of life on my grandfather's small farm in South Buckinghamshire. It was war-time, yet my early childhood seemed wrapped in timeless peace and security. In a world of mortal danger and upheaval, with so many uncertainties, my lowly parents and other grown-ups hid all their fears and troubles by lavishing love upon their little ones. At that time, also, Britain seemed to have a settled sense of purpose in the world, and a still-prevailing view that history, the Empire and ultimately, God himself, were on our side. In May 1940, just a few months before I was born, King George VI had called the nation to prayer, and a very great deliverance had been seen at Dunkirk; also, a few months later, from the aerial onslaught of the 'Battle of Britain'.

Grandad had a few cattle, including a Shorthorn house-cow, a few poultry, and lots of pigs. The pigs were fed on waste-food collected from London's hotels, railway depots and bakeries, just 20 miles away. Strange to say, lots of our cutlery and crockery was salvaged from the swill: a hint of changing attitudes in the workplace, during a time of social upheaval.

Although food was rationed, it was amazing how much was still wasted. A heap of stale loaves gave me a mountain to climb, so high and crusty that I grazed my knees in the process. But when soaked and mixed with the hot swill, it all smelt so good! At feeding time, the pigs' famished squeals would reach a crescendo, silenced only by the thick, nutritious soup topped with barley meal, and poured into the troughs over their hungry snouts.

One of the farm cats had kittens, which I wheeled around in a little wooden barrow, lined with straw. Their names were 'Blackie', 'Ginger' and 'Whisky'. I loved to collect the eggs from the henhouse, but one day, my path was blocked by a pair of geese, nesting in some nettles near the door. They hissed and rose-up, their great wings flapping, until Granddad came to my rescue, and forced a way through. I soon learned respect for the creatures: that is, what you could do, or not do. I didn't go that way again alone; nor disturb Granddad when he was milking the cow. That could mean him being knocked off his stool, and the milk sent flying!

Immediately after lunch, Nana would insist I had 'forty winks' on the chaise-longue, cosseted under a thick tartan blanket. There, as I drifted in and out of sleep, I'd hear the sparrows chattering outside, or the twittering of swallows. For them, too, the farm was a haven of peace, as they nested in the pig sties, sheds and barns. Such sounds and smells, even now, evoke those far-off days of childhood bliss. Thankful though I am for all these memories, and especially for my beloved parents, grandparents and others, I had as yet no conscious awareness of my everlasting refuge: the One who would help me make sense of the great and wonderful world I had been born into.

Happy is that people, that is in such a case: yea, happy is that people, whose God is the LORD.

Psalm 144:15

EARLY DAYS AT HOME AND AT SCHOOL

Sometimes, when I complained about having to go to school, my parents used to say 'school-days are the best days of your life!' I think this was because they'd had to grow up fast and start work very young, certainly by the time they were fourteen years of age.

Most work then was hard and long. My father laboured on a farm, starting at 5.00am: either to milk cows, or to cut kale for them in the winter frost; or to hoe rows of potatoes in the heat of summer, all by hand. It could take all day just to complete one or two rows across a field. He had only one Sunday off a month, and earned very little.

My mother had to do many routine tasks using what little we had. There was a coal-fired stove upon which to cook and heat water, and to keep us warm in winter. Water was from a tap in the garden, and a bath had to be taken in a tin-tub in front of the fire. We also had paraffin stoves and lamps for heating and light. There was no washing machine, no refrigerator and no flush toilet. The wireless (radio) was powered by an 'accumulator', an old-fashioned type of battery which had to be charged at a local garage. One morning, 1st of May 1945, our wireless brought the momentous news: *'Hitler is dead!'* There were many good and happy times, but it was quite a hard life for my dear parents.

Now, about my school days: there's something very important for all children to hear. When you are a child, especially if you are very young, it can be difficult to know what to expect, as you move from one experience to another: a new school, a new class, a new teacher; and what about the other boys and girls? I know that all children can be wonderfully brave when given a little encouragement, but there's no doubt that growing up can be tough at times!

When I was 5 or 6, I found out for the first time that other children can sometimes be very selfish and unkind. They vary, of course, just as adults do. Perhaps they've been bullied by others, so they survive by becoming bullies themselves. If you've been bullied, remember: inside every bully is a coward. Sometimes, perhaps they are really the ones to be pitied!

So it was, when I was about six years old, a family friend gave me a pair of boxing gloves, to encourage me to stand up for myself. I don't think I ever took to them much but it was a kind thought, which boosted my confidence. It's very important for us all to know that when we are picked-on for one reason or another, there's someone on our side. And all who themselves like to be kindly treated, should befriend and support others who are having a difficult time: it might even save their lives. I promise you: one day, you'll be richly rewarded!

One last thing: I remember twin sisters who were in my class at that time. They were both gentle and had lovely blonde hair. However, one was very thin and frail, often too ill to come to school, and we heard that one night she had nearly died. The healthy one told me her sister loved me, as I was big and strong! Sadly, I don't think I was very pleased. Now I know I really should have been…

The name of the LORD is a strong tower: the righteous runneth into it, and is safe.

Proverbs 18:10

HYMN OF CONTENTMENT

He that is down needs fear no fall,
He that is low, no pride;
He that is humble ever shall
Have God to be his guide.

I am content with what I have,
Little be it or much;
And, Lord, contentment, still I crave,
Because Thou savest such.

Fullness to such a burden is
That go on pilgrimage;
Here little, and hereafter bliss,
Is best from age to age.

John Bunyan 1628-88.

John Bunyan was a poor, barely-educated Bedfordshire tinker (a travelling mender of metal pots and pans), who was jailed for twelve years for his faithful preaching. 'The Pilgrim's Progress', his masterly best-known work, was written whilst imprisoned, its message growing like a mighty oak tree. After the Bible, it is one of the most important Christian books to read.

Better is the poor that walketh in his uprightness, than he that is perverse in his ways, though he be rich.

Proverbs 28:6

OF BIRDS AND BOOKS

From the earliest age, I had a great love of the natural world, especially the bird kingdom. Imagine what the world would be like without the joyful sound of birds, their immense variety and beauty, and ability to fly.

Like all young children of those days, I had memorable periods of being unwell with one-off illnesses such as measles, chicken pox and mumps. Such ailments, although commonplace, meant quite a lot of extra care and attention. The doctor would visit and insist on the need for complete rest in a warm bed (few had central heating), plus a nourishing diet, to lessen the risk of complications. Not so long ago, many children had died of diseases like whooping cough and scarlet fever; so in the absence of modern drugs and vaccines, old-fashioned nursing was essential for a safe recovery.

This meant that not only was I excused school, but I received extra love and care from my mother and other dear souls. Chicken was rarely on the menu, so it was a special treat when Mrs Cox, a dear Methodist friend of my grandmother's, brought chicken broth with pearl barley: a delicious soup to help me get better. But this wasn't all: she also used to bring some 'odds-and-ends' as she called them: an assortment of old toys left by her grown-up sons – a few tin soldiers, a 'dinky' model car, a jig-saw puzzle – lots of little things, which were a joy to cheer me on the road to recovery! On one such occasion, my mother bought me a small book about an oak tree, and all the creatures that lived within its great leafy branches. This absorbed me for hours, and greatly inspired me. Mumps was fun, after all!

I went to an ordinary village primary school, with all the usual 'rough-and-tumble' and childhood naughtiness. Although I wasn't aware of being particularly bright, as I look back now, we had some truly remarkable teachers, who had such a passion for drawing out a child's potential.

When I was around nine years old, I built a bird table in the back garden. Starlings were the most frequent visitors, and although such a common bird, in the sunlight their feathers glistened in an array of beautiful colours, making them into something exotic. To my great surprise, and my parents' delight, I was given first prize in my class, comprising a five-shilling 'Observer's Book of British Birds', which was to thrill me for years to come. In the preface, the author mentioned how the Linnet often nests in gorse bushes, and would remain sitting on its young even amidst a heath fire. I remember tearfully reading this to my mother, as she tenderly shared my emotion. Later that year, as a Christmas present, she bought me a larger book called 'British Birds and their Eggs' (Volume 1 was all she could afford). This inspired my escapades in the woods and fields beyond, and set me on a course that would shape my whole future.

Train up a child in the way he should go; and when he is old, he will not depart from it.

Proverbs 22:6

THE SKYLARK

From the way it soars higher and higher, all the while singing, until but a tiny speck in the sky, the skylark is the most inspirational of birds. It seems to sing for sheer joy, rising to 'heaven's gate' as the poets say. Between the deafening sounds of battle on the Western Front in World War I, soldiers in the trenches marvelled at the lark exulting in the skies above them, prompting heart-pangs, beyond their present 'hell', for the bliss of home and heaven.

The lark's shrill strains on a spring morning featured in my own child-hood, and were as common as the chirping of sparrows on the rooftops. Many now couldn't say if they'd ever heard a skylark at all. Sadly, not a few things in the world are like this, and although there's still much that's beautiful, the rich variety familiar to past generations is in decline. Among the trees, the noble elm, which once graced our countryside, is but a memory now.

There was a row of houses near my home called 'Skylark Road', harking back to the open fields where it was built. Several of my primary school friends lived there, all of them characterful in their various ways. Alan was a little shy and less robust than some of the other boys, and of a gentle nature. There came a day when he told us his mother was very ill, and asked if we'd like to go indoors to see her. His father was in the kitchen peeling vegetables, his face hollow-cheeked and lined with cares, and as usual, wearing his trilby *'titfer'* (cockney slang for *'tit-for-tat'*: *hat*!) We followed Alan upstairs, as he quietly took us into his parents' bedroom. Here, his dear mother lay, looking so pale and subdued. Just a few softly-spoken words and a faint smile passed between them, before we ran out to play again. I believe it wasn't long before poor Alan lost his mother.

Being not long after World War II, and penicillin only just discovered, premature death was no stranger to us. Children are at once tender and resilient: and like a calf or a lamb weaned from its mother, there's a lot of pitiful crying at first, but mercifully, the pain subsides, and the business of growing up has to take over. I really didn't take it all in at the time, yet I remember still, how tenderly the dear boy approached his mother that afternoon, long ago. She must have looked up at us from her pillow and wondered how her little son would fare in the world, without her love and care.

Now there stood by the cross of Jesus his mother, and his mother's sister, Mary the wife of Cleophas, and Mary Magdalene. When Jesus therefore saw his mother, and the disciple standing by, whom he loved, he saith unto his mother, Woman, behold thy son! Then saith he to the disciple, Behold thy mother! And from that hour that disciple took her unto his own home.

John 19:25-27

THE COLOUR TURQUOISE-BLUE

One day – I think I was probably about eight or nine years old – I was out with a group of boys, running amok in the hinterland around our new home. We'd moved to a council house on the edge of a village, some 3 miles away. Although so much better for my dear parents, looking back, I can see that an easier life is not, of itself, the secret to permanent happiness. But for me, in my new haunts, there were still many interesting places to explore: a railway station with its archways, tunnels and embankments; waste land awaiting development; fast roads to faraway places; and country lanes, fields and woods.

It would have been a lovely afternoon in late spring, as half a dozen urchins crossed the main road and entered a field edged by a large wood. Little clearings led-off into wide paths, deeper and deeper into the unknown, until they became narrow and all but impenetrable, giving way to a jungle of mossy trees and saplings, with brambles and dead branches under foot.

We came across a small bower, comprising a few slender branches adorned with honeysuckle: a really pretty sight, with the most beautiful scent in the diffused woodland sunlight. A nest was spotted, and its delicate beauty clumsily investigated. The marauders seemed restless, probably because the older boys were soon bored. I was left behind a few moments, and peered in to see for myself. It was made of dried grass and moss woven together, lined with smooth, dried mud. I marvelled at its contents: four eggs of a beautiful clear sky-blue colour, and a smattering of black spots over their rounded ends. 'It's a thrush's nest', someone said.

Later, I looked up the Song Thrush in my *Observer's Book of British Birds*: the one I had unexpectedly won as a prize at school. There I read: *'Eggs 4 or 5, of a beautiful bright turquoise-blue, spotted with black. February – July'*. How wonderful! That moment of discovery in the honeysuckle bower forever defined for me the heavenly colour, *'turquoise-blue'*.

Childhood innocence is such a tender thing, so soon trampled and spoiled in this sad and sinful world. But there is wondrous hope when we realize that Jesus, the Creator himself, said that unless we become as little children, we could in no wise enter the kingdom of heaven. This surely means that all things will eventually be restored, just as they were at the beginning. Of this, dear reader, I have absolutely no doubt – no doubt whatsoever!

Let the field be joyful, and all that is therein: then shall all the trees of the wood rejoice before the LORD: for he cometh, for he cometh to judge the earth: he shall judge the world with righteousness, and the people with his truth.

Psalm 96:12-13

MR FORRESTER AND THE PHEASANT

When I was ten years old, my teacher at school was a Mr Forrester. He was tall, middle-aged, and wore a dark brown suit. His dark hair was combed flat from front to back, and he sported a neat moustache. This, together with his lowering eyes and somewhat haggard expression, gave him a rather fierce look, which went well with his gruff voice and eccentric ways. Like all our teachers in those days, his manner was strict, though tempered with kindness.

For me, this was a time of further discovery and wonder. One autumn evening, I was outside at twilight with my friend Alan, who, with his by-then widowed father, had moved to a new council house in the same street as us. As we looked up at the moon, being a very clear night, we could make out the shadowy outline of its orb, beyond the shining part. There and then, we came to see that it wasn't a flat crescent or circle, but a globe! I was so excited at the discovery, the following day I told Mr Forrester all about it. He patiently listened, and affirmed my deductions. Now that I think about it, he was so kind and encouraging.

On another occasion, I'd spent an evening drawing a pheasant, strutting proudly on the edge of a bluebell wood. This place was the far-side of a meadow, where we'd previously lived when I was about six years old. In that same field was a pond, which I believe was the crater of a stray WW2 bomb. I'd sailed wooden boats there, or collected frog-spawn. Nearby was a gnarled, hollow oak tree, which you could climb-up into on the inside, and come out at the top, among the leaves and acorns! And in a hedge-bottom along the lane, inside a rusty can, some older boys found a Robin's nest with eggs, and later, babies – the first I'd ever seen. As I recalled that idyllic place, it was the perfect setting for my magnificent bird. Next day, I took it to show Mr Forrester. He returned it to me later, with *'V. good, 9½'* neatly penned in red at the bottom of the page.

Recently, as I drove down a fast country road, I saw a beautiful cock pheasant fly across and collide with a van, a short distance ahead. The dear creature was close enough for me to see its look of alarmed innocence, as it bounced off the van and up into the air with feathers flying, before falling to the ground in mortal shock. It was some distance before I could find a place to stop safely, and walk back to check its fate. There it was, lying still on the tarmac. After some cars sped by in their morning haste, I managed to pick it up, and lay it on the verge under a hedge. It was no less beautiful than the pheasant I'd drawn as a child.

They shall not hurt nor destroy in all my holy mountain: for the earth shall be full of the knowledge of the LORD, as the waters cover the sea.

Isaiah 11:9

LILIES OF THE VALLEY

Plants and animals depend upon each other in a wonderful way. Plants provide us with food, medicine, building materials and a beautiful environment. They also purify the air, by turning the carbon dioxide that everything breathes out into food, whilst replenishing the oxygen; other animal waste, with the help of small creatures such as worms and bacteria, enriches the soil for the plants.

My passion for growing things began very early. As a six-year-old, I saw some little plants growing by a stream, and thinking them to be lilies, took them home to transplant around a small pond I had made for some tadpoles, which were now turning into baby frogs.

Food was still rationed as we emerged from World War II, so that we grew lots of potatoes, even in the front garden! Hoeing up the rows in the heat of summer was exhausting, and I asked my Dad how he managed to do this, out in the fields all day long. 'You get used to it', he said, gently and thoughtfully.

Later, in my early teens, I branched out into growing lettuces, tomatoes and cucumbers, the surplus being purchased by kind neighbours who wanted to encourage my efforts. In my idealism, I'd always wanted to be a farmer, but my grandparents knew it to be a hard life. By the time I was sixteen, I realized it was the natural world that drew me, rather than the hard-headed realities of farming. Passionate in my study of chemistry, botany and zoology, I decided to pursue a career in veterinary science. This seemed a good way of combining all my interests, although my decision was perhaps based on necessity rather than aptitude. Probably most young people have to compromise a little, in choosing what to do with their lives, and how best to earn a living.

In later years, as retirement approached, I returned to my gardening, which gave me great delight. Despite successes and failures, my childhood skills revived, and using natural methods wherever possible, I was able to grow a wide range of vegetables and fruit. The raising of crops and livestock is good for body, mind and spirit, and perhaps it's for this reason I found such a sense of kinship, affection and respect for the farming folk I worked among.

In the Bible, man's journey starts in the Garden of Paradise, and is restored in Christ's Kingdom. The Song of Solomon is a potent picture of the love between Christ and his faithful Bride (all those who, by faith, truly know and love him). The theme is gloriously portrayed in the Old Testament Prophets, and also in the New Testament. Meanwhile, God's people were shepherds, perfected through the rugged life of the hill country, rather than the fertile fields of the lowlands. But the prophet Isaiah foretells that, one day, as God again delights in his estranged people, the whole land of Israel will be *Hephzi-bah*, meaning *'my delight is in her'* and *'Beulah'*, meaning *'Married'*: becoming as green and fruitful as Eden.

In the midst of the street of it, and on either side of the river, was there the tree of life, which bare twelve manner of fruits, and yielded her fruit every month: and the leaves of the tree were for the healing of the nations.

Revelation 22:2

BIRDS' NESTS

Each kind of bird has its own type of nest, nesting habits and egg colouration. Among country boys there was great delight, and often skill, too, in finding a nest, observing its contents and seeing the fledglings grow till they were able to fly. In my own boyhood, this led to many adventures, some quite dangerous: we crawled into thorn hedges, climbed great trees, reached into holes and crossed rivers and lakes, to name but a few of our escapades.

Ground-nesting birds such as Skylarks, Meadow Pipits, Peewits, and Partridges presented a special challenge, because they were so good at hiding their simple nests through camouflaged plumage, egg colouration and deceiving antics. No bird would drop down to the exact spot where its nest lay. Rather, it would alight some distance away, then secretively run along the ground. If you approached a Peewit's nest, the parent birds would flap around nearby, feigning injury, so that the intruder would be distracted and drawn away after them.

One of my school-friends, despite living in a large industrial town, rode out into the countryside on his bicycle whenever he could. Being small, his nickname was Willie, and apart from being very good at maths, he had very keen powers of observation. One day, as he gazed out of a classroom window across a courtyard, he saw a pair of Pied Wagtails high up on the school roof. There were some old desks parked along the wall of the courtyard below, of the type that had sloping wooden lids and a hole for an inkwell along the top. Willie spotted what no-one else had noticed: the Wagtails were swooping down and popping through an inkwell hole! Later, we took a discrete look inside the desk, to find the normally inaccessible nest of a Pied Wagtail.

It's very hard to find a Cuckoo's nest, or rather, a nest of another bird in which a Cuckoo has substituted an egg of her own. But Willie managed it: he found a Robin's nest which had received an alien visit! The single, large, fluffy, Cuckoo chick had already ousted and out-grown the duped Robins' own chicks. The adoptive parents worked tirelessly to feed their guest for free, whilst the true parents took an early flight back to Africa. This bizarre 'brood parasitism', for all its skulduggery, is at every stage an awesome and intricate miracle.

What is the purpose of such weird and wonderful works of nature? One thing we can say for sure, is that in all its immense variety and beauty, a balance has been maintained over centuries past. But do they not also speak to us at a deeper level? King Solomon, who lived a thousand years before Christ, was greatly blessed with wisdom, and wrote much about the natural world. In the biblical book of Ecclesiastes, we read that he tried in vain to fathom it all. Sadly, despite all the favour God had shown him, he strayed greatly in later life. Wisdom, wealth and knowledge alone, are not enough to satisfy the longing soul.

That their hearts might be comforted, being knit together in love, and unto all riches of the full assurance of understanding, to the acknowledgement of the mystery of God, and of the Father, and of Christ; in whom are hid all the treasures of wisdom and knowledge.

Colossians 2:2-3

A TRIBUTE TO GOD'S TRUE SERVANTS

Like many children of my age, I was brought up in the Christian faith. Our parents and grandparents encouraged us to pray as little children. At school, we were taught the Lord's Prayer and various stories from the Bible, sang hymns in morning assemblies, and gave thanks to God for our food. Whilst I'm sure it was good we were taught these things, they didn't become real to me until much later. Even so, this Protestant Christian influence benefited us at many levels, for it was the unseen foundation of our national way of life: take away this wonderful heritage, and you could be sure we wouldn't be the blessed and happy people we once were.

As I look back now, apart from our parents and teachers, there was another very important group of people. These were the ones for whom the Christian faith was a *living reality*. It motivated everything they did, and their hearts beat with the love of Jesus everywhere they went. They would always be ready to speak about him to anyone who would listen, especially to us children. It's only now I can look back and see each one standing along life's journey, pointing to him who is *'the Way, the Truth and the Life'*. Though seldom heard, they led by both word and example; and when all seemed in vain, they fended for us unseen, through their prayers.

In my early teens, I was overcome with tears when I heard the evangelist Billy Graham on TV. He said that *my* sins had been responsible for Jesus' death on the Cross, and this cut me to the heart, so that I wept in sorrow. Although I soon got over it, I'm sure my reaction did not go unnoticed in heaven above.

Like many my age in those days, I attended a Church of England Sunday School class. We older boys were taught by a dear godly gentleman called Mr Kidner. Each week, we'd be issued with a coloured picture-stamp with a Bible text. The stamp would be stuck into a booklet, and we'd have to look up the text at home, memorize it and recite it in class, for which Mr Kidner would give each of us a mark. Although I was quite diligent, it was as if I was like those in the parable of the sower, in whom none of the seed took root. We were encouraged to go along to church once a month, but I think I only went once, as the formal religion of the adult world simply didn't mean anything to me.

By the time I was fifteen, my worldview was turned upside down through my interest in science, and the exciting appeal of the Theory of Evolution. In my youthful folly, I began to see all traditional religion as a huge pretence, and so I stopped going to Mr Kidner's Bible Class. A few months later, I met him in the village whilst shopping for my mother, and in his usual gentle way, he asked me why they hadn't seen me for a while. I had to explain that I would not be true to myself, now that I had a new-found scientific understanding of everything! Dear Mr Kidner: I don't think I ever saw him again, although we did receive some pastoral follow-up on the issues I'd raised, both at home and at school. It's only now that I realize how wonderful it is that the true servants of God, in their weakness and suffering of the scorn and rejection that Jesus suffered, yet availed much for us in prayer.

For though he was crucified through weakness, yet he liveth by the power of God. For we also are weak in him, but we shall live with him by the power of God toward you.

2 Corinthians 13:4

THIS SCEPTRED ISLE

A school friend and I, wanting to practise our language skills, embarked on an ambitious bicycle tour across Europe. Staying overnight in youth hostels, we cycled from our homes in Buckinghamshire, first to Dover, thence by ferry to Ostend. From there, we cycled across Belgium, Holland and into Germany, up the Rhine Valley to Freiburg and the Black Forest beyond, not far from Switzerland; from thence we returned home through northern France, Luxembourg, and Belgium, the whole 1200-mile trip being completed in under three weeks. At seventeen, we were pretty fit!

Looking back now, one realizes that many other young men, many not much older, had twice fought for our freedom across these same lands, not so many years before. I remember, on a couple of occasions, seeing a small headstone in a wayside hedgerow under a tree, marking the grave of a soldier. I think these were probably later removed to the main official cemeteries in France and the Low Countries, where many, many thousands of servicemen were laid to rest. How terrible the cost; how fragile the peace!

Such a lot has happened since those days: atomic bombs dropped on Japan; the partition of Germany and Europe by an 'Iron Curtain'; the Korean war, dividing the country into two; and a 'Cold War' between East and West; then, with the decline of Communism in the late 1980's, the re-unification of Germany, and liberation of East European countries, to join the European Union. Meanwhile, on 14th May 1948, after the holocaust in which some six million Jews perished under the Nazis, the modern state of Israel was born – the first time that descendants of Jacob had directly governed part of their ancient homeland since the exile to Babylon, over 2,500 years before. Since then, many attempts by their enemies to dislodge them led to Israeli control being extended, even to Jerusalem, that great city of Jewish yearning, upon which all eyes are now focused.

We might wonder why Britain was spared the worst horrors of these wars in Europe, though not forgetting the aerial warfare that wreaked destruction upon our cities, taking many innocent lives; nor the great sacrifices made by so many brave servicemen. We should remember too, the vast numbers on both sides caught up in hostilities, who in truth, would rather have been men of peace. But once the forces behind the pride of nations is unleashed, everyone has to do their duty. My father worked on the land, with a German Prisoner-of-War as a work-mate. At that level, I saw guarded acts of kindness pass between them. So what was it all about, and why did the war have to happen?

First, the leaders of the nations must protect their citizens and allies from evil and aggression. These things are a reality in this world, and the cost of withstanding them will often be high. But for the full answer to this question, we must understand the deeper truths of Scripture. This much we can now say, and soberly reflect upon: though it be through the influence of but a few, the extent to which a nation responds to, or rejects, the grace of God, is eventually out-worked in its history.

And when ye shall hear of wars and rumours of wars, be ye not troubled: for such things must needs be; but the end shall not be yet.

Mark 13:7

CLAPHAM JUNCTION

It's all change at Clapham Junction,
With Lavender Hill in view;
My 'old kit-bag' at the ready,
To alight at Waterloo!

Many go to and fro from here,
As they did in ages past;
Young men in uniform to fight,
The bravest to the last.

What made Britain special,
This Sceptred Isle so fair?
What made the Marian Martyrs burn,
Their light for Christ to bear?

Holy hearts that beat like pumps,
Pure water of life prepared:
Clouds of witnesses on high,
The Gospel to the world declared!

As the years have passed,
It's not enough to rest on laurels green;
For the sap runs dry and the colour fades,
Where Truth's Lifeblood had been.

(Upon the approach of the EU Referendum, Spring 2016.)

Personal photograph taken at 'Shropshire Lavender',
Wellbank Farm, Pickstock, Newport.

Righteousness exalteth a nation: but sin is a reproach to any people.

Proverbs 14:34

SACRED COW

Long ago, when I was still a young and inexperienced vet, I was called to assist a colleague with an abdominal operation on a cow. Sadly, there were complications, and it was decided the animal would have to be put down. As we didn't have the special gun with us, I was to fetch it as soon as possible and finish the job, whilst my colleague packed up our equipment and went home.

What I'm about to relate may seem strange. You might think that any qualified person would carry this out without a second thought. But this was the first time I'd ever used a gun, and the first time I'd ever destroyed such a magnificent and noble creature. On the way back to the farm I felt nervous, with an inexplicable dread. I stopped at a lay-by and found myself, literally, weak at the knees. What happened next was extraordinary. I was, at that time, still an atheist: yet I bowed my head and prayed that God would forgive me for what I was about to do, and help me to do it efficiently.

The cow was already chained-up in her stall, so the farmer could discretely withdraw. Stockmen who've reared animals from birth are often emotionally affected at times like this; probably, also, it was best to get out of the way for safety reasons! I was no doubt pleased to be left alone, in case I appeared hand-fisted, or anything went wrong. I loaded the gun and, speaking softly and apologetically to the cow, placed the barrel over the appropriate spot, hoping she wouldn't move at the last moment. A sharp knock on the firing pin, and the great beast went straight down where she stood. A huge sense of relief came over me, mixed with sadness and awe: I had done it, and it had gone well: her suffering was over.

I think many a soldier will identify with this. The British Army, in time of war, had to help conscripts overcome a reluctance to use their weapons against the enemy. I have also heard it said that war is 99% boredom and 1% sheer terror; and that there are no atheists on the battlefield! Of course, in time, we tend to become hardened. In later life, I had to do such tasks often, and train others to do them. But the experience of that first occasion never really left me.

Personal photograph by kind permission of owners, Mr & Mrs Francis

But to this man will I look, even to him that is poor and of a contrite spirit, and trembleth at my word. He that killeth an ox is as if he slew a man;

Isaiah 66:2b-3a

IMPRISONED SPIRIT

When one considers all the wonders of nature, how strange it is that so many are content to see it all as a meaningless cosmic accident, of which we are a hapless part. After the mystery of the Creation itself, here is another: the wilful blindness of intelligent, sophisticated humanity.

Indeed, I was once such a person, denying all that pointed to the existence of a Creator. The tender heart I grew up with had become hardened, and I revelled instead in ideas which had an appearance of being plausible, but when closely weighed, left much to be desired. Why did I follow such a path? I doubt I really knew at the time. I think it came with the rejection of what I saw as closed-minded religion, and my own unwillingness to be morally accountable. More than that: in truth, I was simply *spiritually* dead, and couldn't help myself any more than if I'd been physically dead. Trying to bring such a person to life was no more effective than trying to warm-up a corpse. Nothing came of such efforts, until the candle of my spirit was re-kindled by God's Spirit.

A wonderful day came when I walked out of darkness, and into the light. In fact, it was a process, rather than a single event on a single day, as the little flame that the Spirit of God had kindled, gradually grew in strength. When the words of the early chapters of John's Gospel registered in my spirit, I *believed*: and as I did so, I knew something had happened within.

I had studied the natural sciences and knew many dry facts, which were all hung on a great rickety fence that imprisoned my soul. Now, in the light of God's word, and with the help of a book I was led to*, I was able to see the evidence for life's origins from a renewed perspective. A breach was made in that great fence, and as I escaped into the glorious light of Spring-time, I worshipped God, weeping for joy. Everything had a meaning after all, and the words of so many hymns became suddenly real to me!

To be fair, it's perfectly reasonable that we should have many questions. The Creation itself is only the first 'Book': but we must go to another, more perfect Book, to get the full picture. Only then, with the help of the Spirit of God in Christ Jesus (without whom many err in their interpretation), shall we begin to understand it all. Here, we learn that the original Creation was perfect in every way, unfettered by sin and death, as it is now. But God had foreseen everything from the beginning, and made provision for a glorious redemption through his Son. We also discover that Jesus the Messiah will come to reign as rightful King from his throne in Jerusalem, that very city where once he suffered and died in our place, as the spotless Lamb of God: AND ALL WILL BE RESTORED!

* *'Evolution or Creation?' Prof H Enoch, 1967, Evangelical Press (out of print). But there are many excellent resources now available, that provide scientific support for Genesis. They affirm that the Universe is not billions of years old, the impossibility of evolution as an explanation for the Creation, the reality of the Flood of Noah and the logistics of the ark and its cargo. Sources I have used include the Creation Science Movement, Portsmouth, England, Creation Ministries International, and Biblical Creation Trust. God's word, and Christ's once-for-all work on the Cross, are sufficient to bring us to a saving faith; but such is the attack on the truth of the Bible in our times, I believe these ministries are a special mercy from God. Biblical prophecy and events in the Holy Land provide another supporting evidence that the Bible is historically trustworthy. But for now, as Paul wrote to the believers at Corinth: '...I determined not to know any thing among you, save Jesus Christ, and him crucified'*

For ye were as sheep going astray; but are now returned unto the Shepherd and Bishop of your souls.

1 Peter 2:25

A CREATION HYMN

All things bright and beautiful,
All creatures great and small,
All things wise and wonderful,
The Lord God made them all. (Chorus)

Each little flower that opens,
Each little bird that sings,
He made their glowing colours,
He made their tiny wings.

The rich man in his castle,
The poor man at his gate,
God made them high and lowly,
And ordered their estate.

The purple headed mountain,
The river running by,
The sunset and the morning,
That brightens up the sky;

The cold wind in the winter,
The pleasant summer sun,
The ripe fruits in the garden,
He made them every one:

The tall trees in the greenwood,
The meadows where we play,
The rushes by the water,
We gather every day;

He gave us eyes to see them,
And lips that we might tell,
How great is God Almighty,
Who has made all things well.
Cecil Frances Alexander, 1823-95 (original version).

Many, O LORD my God, are thy wonderful works which thou hast done, and thy thoughts which are to us-ward: they cannot be reckoned up in order unto thee: if I would declare and speak of them, they are more than can be numbered.

Psalm 40:5

OF ANIMALS & MAN

Everyone has a fascination for animals. But just as human relationships are often complex and difficult, so it is with the creatures. Despite an overall harmony, there's a tension between what is ideal and what is real. Such contradictions are the root cause of much conflict and heartache.

For example, we all love our pets, with their innocence, affection and loyalty. Yet we exploit and kill countless millions of equally beautiful creatures for food and clothing. A vet treats sick animals, yet at the same time, has also to carry out hurtful and destructive procedures. The only consolation is to ensure such duties are done as humanely as possible.

There's but one Book that makes sense of these perplexities; and but one Man who'll bring all our sorrows to an end. Genesis, the first book of the Bible, reveals a time when the first man, Adam, was in perfect harmony with the creatures, giving them all names. There was no death, and their food was only herbs, seeds and fruit. After the curse of rebellion against God blighted the Creation, the world became a very different place; and with the new beginning after the great Flood of Noah's day, the world was again, much altered. It was then that God decreed that thereafter, animals could be killed for food.

As to the Man, the 'Second Adam', we see the first hint of him in Genesis. How could the ancient writer have known, unless he'd had the divine insight of a prophet? For there we discern the Seed of the woman, who'd bruise the Serpent's head. And in mercy, God himself clothed Adam and Eve, before banishing them from Eden: he made them coats of skins from animals sacrificed on their behalf, foreshadowing the Passover Lamb on the cross.

The saving purpose of the Most High can therefore be discerned right from the beginning. Through the obedience of his faithful Son, Jesus Christ, we too would be provided with a covering before a holy God, namely, a *'robe of righteousness'*. This was no myth: it happened right there in Jerusalem, under the eyes of the Romans. The day is coming when the Creator, *'in whom we live and move and have our being'*, will judge the world in righteousness by that Man of Calvary: and he's given assurance of this to all, by raising him from the dead. The *'slain Lamb'* will then be recognised as *'the Lion of the Tribe of Judah'*.

Do you see then, dear reader, how this makes sense of all we experience in our relationship to other forms of life, as well as to one another? For the whole creation was subjected to futility, and awaits the hope of redemption in Christ, just as we do. Perhaps you barely see it now: but once you have put your trust in God's only begotten Son, the Spirit (the 'Interpreter') will guide you into *'all the truth'*.

The wolf also shall dwell with the lamb, and the leopard shall lie down with the kid; and the calf and the young lion and the fatling together; and a little child shall lead them. And the cow and the bear shall feed; their young ones shall lie down together: and the lion shall eat straw like the ox. And the sucking child shall play on the hole of the asp, and the weaned child shall put his hand on the cockatrice' den. They shall not hurt nor destroy in all my holy mountain: for the earth shall be full of the knowledge of the LORD, as the waters cover the sea.

Isaiah 11:6-9

WHAT'S A GOOD VET?

I used to visit a certain livestock auction, where there was a large corrugated iron shed for the sale of produce and smaller livestock. There were rows of cages for the chickens and other poultry, and at certain times of the year, there would be orphan lambs, too. It was a motley selection of creatures, as were the country folk who gathered there weekly to buy and sell. As you may imagine, the place had its own distinctive cacophony of sounds, sights and smells.

My role was to make sure the livestock were healthy and fit for sale, and to ensure they were treated with reasonable care. On a hot day, for example, I'd insist that drinking water was replenished, and as far as possible, ensure that the building was kept well ventilated. Much as I'm fond of country folk, I've observed a certain hardness takes over when market forces are at work, and it was down to me to uphold a decent standard of care.

Being a professional of any kind can lead to a sense of inadequacy. The more one knows, the more one realizes how little one knows. With the passage of time and the gaining of experience, a measure of confidence may be attained. But one is always aware of the gap between what is, and what could be. In my experience, it's at this point the man of faith instinctively reaches within, seeking the help of the Creator of all things.

From what I have written already, my readers will know that I hadn't always known this blessed connection. There came a time, as a young man, when out of an inner void, I was drawn to that immortal, invisible, and only-wise God who I'd vaguely known about in my child-hood. A personal calling, over a period of time, led to a place where a perfect, spotless Lamb was found – one who'd been slain in my place, atoning for all my inadequacies, failures and wrong-doings. That Lamb had paid the blood-price, enabling me to walk free, with nothing separating me from the love of God! From that time on, I knew there was *'a very present help'* in time of need. *'What would you have me to do, Lord?'* I had asked, expecting to be sent onto the mission field, or into the ministry of the Church. But no: *'Do your work well'*, was his gentle command. And when difficulties reared-up to daunt or discourage, the golden words *'I will help you'* were intoned in my heart. Looking back now, so many imperfections in his unworthy yoke-fellow were smoothed-over and sanctified.

The man who looked after the Poultry and Produce section at the auction was a great animal lover. A retired schoolmaster, he was kind and gentle, and seemed more than a little out of place in that raucous 'Vanity Fair'. Rabbits were also sold there – dead or alive – and he told me of one that had escaped, taking refuge in some dark corner under the cages. It was never caught, so he brought it food each day for a long while afterwards. One very humbling remark of his I'll never forget: 'To me', he said, 'the veterinary profession is the noblest of all.'

And whatsoever ye do, do it heartily, as to the LORD, and not unto men.

Colossians 3:23

HORSES FOR COURSES

It was during my days in private practice that I'd seen, and come to, the Light. This was when I first heard that simple word of guidance: *'Do your work well'*. But how? There were aspects I didn't find at all easy. What was I to do about 'horsey' work, for instance? Some would love working with horses: or more precisely, with the horsey world; but I'm afraid I wasn't one of them!

Within quite a short time, I was called one Sunday afternoon to a pony that was suffering from 'colic'. It belonged to the daughter of a famous person in the racing world, and was being looked after by a lady who ran a local livery stable. Horses are very prone to colic, because their digestive tract is very narrow at one point. Normally, the treatment was to give laxatives, warm bran mashes and muscle relaxant drugs, and in many cases, it would resolve after a few hours. Meanwhile, the horse would have to be walked around to discourage it from rolling, as it was believed this might lead to a rapidly fatal intestinal torsion.

As nightfall approached, and the poor creature's condition worsened, I knew that surgery was the only hope. However, equine abdominal surgery was rarely attempted by general practitioners, and without immediate access to a veterinary hospital with specialist facilities, it seemed I was on my own. Returning to base, I assembled the instruments, and hurriedly read up on the appropriate sedation and anaesthesia. By chance, I'd recently found an article about a certain drug that had been trialled in horses. This enabled me to narcotise the pony in the standing position, and block the nerves to the flank using local anaesthetic: a procedure we often used in cattle.

With the assistance of the stable lady as nurse, I worked through the night, probing the abdominal contents through a vertical flank incision of about 10 inches. Amazingly, the brave little pony stood sleepily for hours during the whole procedure, with little sign of pain. Eventually, I found an impacted ileum – that narrow portion of the equine intestinal tract. But the hard, pelleted contents wouldn't budge, so I had to excise them by cutting into the bowel. All of a sudden, as I removed the pellets one by one, there was a huge gush of 'trapped wind'. Our patient looked visibly relieved, as were my helper and I! The long job of stitching-up followed, ensuring the bowel incision was closed without causing too much further narrowing. As the start of another week dawned, it was time for breakfast, and off to Tb-test 200 cattle before lunch!

The pony made a marvellous recovery. His owner was so impressed, he asked me to describe my technique to two top equine vets. A year or so later, he kindly wrote to inform me the patient, now thirteen years-old and on a daily supplement of chopped carrots and bran mash, continued to win gymkhana events.

Later, I remembered: I'd told the Lord I found certain areas of work utterly daunting: how could I *'do them well'*? But just as he'd promised in that 'still small voice' of the Spirit within, I saw that he had indeed helped me!

In all thy ways acknowledge him, and he shall direct thy paths.

Proverbs 3:6

LIVING LESSONS

Although much good was done to me by others as I grew up, and I in turn was given opportunity to do the same, it would be wrong to deny my many failings and short-comings. It is a true saying of Christ's, that he hadn't come to call the righteous, but sinners to repentance. But of course, it is also true, in the words of the apostle Paul, that *'all have sinned, and come short of the glory of God'*.

A short time after I'd come to a living faith in him as my personal Saviour, many lessons were to follow. Old things had passed away, and all things had become new. I began to know the blessing of God in every area of my life. But at the same time, I experienced opposition from that same spirit which was in Cain in relation to his brother Abel: for I found it still to be at large in the world, and even in me. The desire to please and to impress dies hard, leading to envy and conflict. The sinful nature of the old Adam lingers on in our hearts, and by the grace of God in Christ, must be mortified, that is, put to death!

Cows have four stomachs, and there's a condition where the fourth stomach can become displaced. As the digestive system fails, the animal grows thin, sickens, and may eventually die. Two methods may be used to correct the problem: one is to bring the animal down with ropes and roll it over, so that the displaced stomach moves back into position of its own accord. The other is a tricky surgical operation done under local anaesthetic, with the cow in the standing position.

I had such a case, and reluctantly, decided to operate. But somehow, I wasn't fully convinced I needed to put the poor creature through it all, so I arranged to have a final look at her the following morning. A younger colleague was to join me about half an hour later, bringing the surgical instruments with him. But as I approached the farm, I had a sense that something wasn't right. It concerned my heart-attitude towards the young colleague, who was very competitive and 'go ahead'. Was I right to feel the way I did? Probably not! Either way, I knew that a holy God could not bless our efforts, with such a thing going on in my heart. Before arriving, therefore, I asked God to forgive me, and to bless the young vet who was about to join me. A great load lifted off my shoulders, and as I drove up to the farm, I sensed all would be well.

The cow stood tied in her stall, and as the farmer and I leant over the door and quietly observed her, I fancied she looked somewhat better. Once I had examined her, I found the fourth stomach had come back into place and was beginning to function normally. To my delight, the operation was no longer necessary!

I'm not claiming this was a miracle, for such cases can occasionally recover of their own accord. But as to the operation that the Holy Spirit had conducted in my heart, that was a certainty, as well I knew. It's sobering to reflect how much sadness and sorrow is brought about in our lives by the sin that clings like death. It taints others around us, and indeed the whole creation is affected, too. No wonder when Jesus comes to reign, there'll be such great blessing and rejoicing!

Personal photograph by kind permission of Mr & Mrs Francis, of happy cows turned out to grass in Spring. The joyful twittering of recently returned swallows filled the air, as one seen here swoops towards them!

For the earnest expectation of the creature waiteth for the manifestation of the sons of God.

Romans 8:19

HYMN – THE COMING KING

Sing we the King who is coming to reign,
Glory to Jesus, the Lamb that was slain.
Life and salvation His empire shall bring,
Joy to the nations when Jesus is King.

Refrain:

Come let us sing, praise to our King,
Jesus our King, Jesus our King,
This is our song, who to Jesus belong:
Glory to Jesus, to Jesus our King.

All men shall dwell in His marvelous light,
Races long severed His love shall unite,
Justice and truth from His sceptre shall spring,
Wrong shall be ended when Jesus is King.

All shall be well in His kingdom of peace,
Freedom shall flourish and wisdom increase,
Foe shall be friend when His triumph we sing,
Sword shall be sickle when Jesus is King.

Souls shall be saved from the burden of sin,
Doubt shall not darken His witness within,
Hell hath no terrors, and death hath no sting;
Love is victorious when Jesus is King.

Kingdom of Christ, for thy coming we pray,
Hasten, O Father, the dawn of the day
When this new song Thy creation shall sing,
Satan is vanquished, and Jesus is King.

Charles S Horne c. 1910

And in mercy shall the throne be established: and he shall sit upon it in truth in the tabernacle of David, judging, and seeking judgment, and hasting righteousness.

Isaiah 16:5

OUR FAITHFUL FRIENDS

What is it about animals, in particular the domesticated kind, that so fascinates us? Whether it's a pet, a flock or a herd, there's a peculiar bond that exists between us and the creatures. The animals differ from us essentially in one thing: although, like young children, they may be trained to do either right or wrong, they are not morally accountable through conscience, in the way that we are. Even when they do nasty things to us, it isn't because of hatred or guile: it's simply how they are, as part of a fallen creation.

It seems we have a need to love and nurture other creatures, which at its best, is enriching and fulfilling; and at its worst, is controlling and abusive. But even the best relationship involves give and take. Where the creatures give up their freedom into human hands, they receive protection, feeding and care. There's a substantial cost in both directions, and always, in the end, a parting. Whether it's the death of a pet, or the necessary trading of livestock for food or other purposes, as in all things in this world, there's joy and delight, but also heartache and sorrow. I've seen many poignant examples of this bittersweet relationship.

Let it be said that nothing is stupid! All creatures have their own typical behaviours, but with individual variations. In general, each kind has its own character-type, marking out its place in the great scheme of things. For example, some are solitary, whilst others flock together. Dogs and horses are inclined to be faithful; donkeys and mules stubborn; cats aloof; rabbits mischievous; foxes sly; badgers creatures-of-habit; rats and mice industrious (to say the least!) Within their own sphere of being, I have found them all extremely knowing.

Consider also the bird kingdom: the gentle dove, the scavenging crow, the watchful hawk, the sociable sparrow; the mimicking parrot, the wily owl. And if we consider the lowlier creatures, we see everything intent on its business, especially the bees and the ants: all is purposeful and full of wisdom. We should consider them all with awe. Their ways are all part of a wonderful revelation, as vast as the number of stars in the sky! But remarkably, when kept in close contact with man, they take on a canny friendship with him; and there's no doubt they know how to respond to love and kindness. This gives us a little glimpse of what the original Creation was like. After all, the Creator himself *is love*.

Which of us isn't moved by the story of a dog that refuses to move from his master's grave? Or the sight of a pet that suffers just as we do? Besides the breath of life, and a self-awareness of their own, do they also have souls? We need light from another source to answer this. In that light, we see not only the 'how' and the 'why', but the ultimate brightness and beauty of all things. We see the express handiwork and character of God in Christ, albeit only dimly at first. But the Creator who brought them all to Adam in the beginning, is able to restore them in his new creation.

All things were created by him, and for him: and he is before all things, and by him all things consist.

Colossians 1:16b-17

THE MAN AND HIS WHIPPET

This is a story from my days in private practice. A man worked as a driver for a local firm of livestock hauliers, and judging by his accent and features, came from the Scottish Borders area. I'd sometimes seen him at livestock markets, or at the farm from which the haulage firm operated.

He was tall, wiry and rough-shaven, and strode about in studded boots, always too busy to stop to talk. No doubt he'd been brought up to work hard, and was not given to showing his feelings too much.

His job entailed loading cattle and sheep onto his large double-decker truck, and although I doubt he could afford to think too deeply about it, it's fair to say his role as a livestock haulier involved a lot of skill. The animals had to be loaded and unloaded in a manner that got the job done, but without leading to injury or bruising. His huge truck had to be manoeuvred into all sorts of awkward places, before being driven the length and breadth of the land in a way that didn't put the live cargo at risk from cornering too sharply, or braking too hard. There's no doubt this was, and is, a very skilled job that few of us would be at home with, and should be accorded the respect it deserves.

One day – I think it was a Saturday morning – the man arrived quite unexpectedly at the surgery. He was carrying in his arms a whippet, a breed of dog which is like a small greyhound. In his usual abrupt 'Borders' accent, he wasted no time in telling me what was to be done with his forlorn little travel companion. He didn't want her to suffer, and the expression on the faces of them both was enough to convince me there was to be no argument. I took the frail little form into the ops room, and with the help of a nurse to hold her for me, she was given an intravenous injection to put her to sleep. The veins on a whippet stand out very well, so the whole procedure was soon quietly and humanely done, as we laid her out on her blanket in an open cardboard box.

Waiting near the entrance to the surgery, the man was his usual restless self. He'd wanted to take back the body for burial, and as I walked up the corridor, some words of comfort came onto my tongue. I hardly expected him to know or appreciate them, yet I felt compelled to express them. I simply said, with a gentle smile, *'The Lord knows even when a sparrow falls'*. Immediately, he hoarsely exclaimed, with a great lump in his throat, *'Tha's godliness thad is…tha's real godliness!'* He hurried away, not wanting to say any more. It was enough for both of us.

I believe the love of Jesus touched the dear man that day. It was as if something from long ago surfaced within him, perhaps from his childhood: something very deep and precious, that was otherwise inexpressible.

Are not two sparrows sold for a farthing? and one of them shall not fall on the ground without your Father.

Matthew 10:29

THE GOOD SHEPHERD

I was once called to attend a large pet sheep, which was owned by a tall, dignified Irishman. I think he'd probably had her since she was a little orphan lamb. She lived at the top of his garden in a small paddock, and whenever he was at home, she followed him everywhere.

The ewe was suffering from a condition well-known to shepherds, called 'garget', which is a most unpleasant form of infection in the milk gland. The whole udder and surrounding under-belly turns black with gangrene, becomes cold to the touch and sloughs away, leaving a large area of raw flesh. If the animal is not attended to, the flies then lay their eggs on the wound, and the poor creature is soon in big trouble, and will die.

I had to visit this dear animal several times, giving her antibiotic injections and applying copious amounts of a bright yellow insecticidal and antiseptic cream. The owner helped by continuing the applications day after day for a long period. In the end, I'm glad to say his loving patience and dedication were rewarded, as the huge wound healed-up and the dear creature fully recovered.

I think it was at my last visit, that I quoted a verse of Scripture to the man. It was from the Gospel of John, Chapter 10, verse 14, and began: *'I am the good shepherd, and know my sheep...'* Before I could finish, the man completed it with a lovely smile, saying, in his charming Irish lilt: *'...and am known of mine!'* Neither of us said any more: those few words brought a perfect meeting of hearts and minds. I sense he knew that his love for his pet ewe, reflected the Saviour's love for his own sheep, whom he knows and calls by name.

It is at times like this, that we all feel grateful for the mercies of medicine and care. Jesus spoke of it in his parable of the Good Samaritan. Upon finding a man mugged and left for dead on the road to Jericho, he turned aside, tended to his wounds, carried him on his donkey, and took the poor fellow to an inn, where he could be taken care of till he recovered. Before going on his way, the Samaritan paid for the man's keep, promising that upon his return he'd repay the inn-keeper whatever more it might cost to bring him back to health.

There are many deep lessons in this parable, which are a great comfort to us. The story reveals exactly what God expects of us when we meet such situations. You must understand that Jews and Samaritans didn't like each other very much, both for historical and religious reasons. Whilst those reasons were understandable from a human point of view, Jesus showed us clearly, that to fulfil the commandment to *'love our neighbour as ourselves'*, he expects us to do as the Samaritan did, even to those who aren't our friends.

Be ye therefore merciful, as your Father also is merciful.

Luke 6:36

HENRIETTA HEN

In my early days in large animal practice, cows were usually tied up in long sheds, in either a single or double row, with a passageway behind and in front. If a vet had to attend a lame hind foot, it wasn't safe to simply walk up to the cow and lift its leg over his knee, as might be done with a well-mannered horse. Try this with a cow, and likely as not, she'd kick you twice before you even felt it! Such kicks were very forceful, and could send you flying across the shed and into the wall. Perhaps only a nasty bruise might result, but it could be far more serious if such a forceful knock landed on one's knee or head.

In order to relieve the poor animal of its pain, the affected foot and lower limb had first to be raised off the ground, so that a thorough examination could be made. One way of doing this was to fold a hessian sack lengthwise, threading one end between the leg and the udder, to meet the other end just above the animal's hock. The ends of the sack were then tightly lassoed in the end of a rope or halter, the other end being hoisted-up over a beam, so that the cow's foot was lifted well clear of the ground.

The problem might simply be a stone wedged between the claws of the hoof; or something sharp stuck in the sole; or an infection around the skin of the heel. Often, a piece of grit was found to have lodged in the seam where the wall and sole joined, and this could lead to a painful abscess in the soft tissues inside the hoof. It was always satisfying to find this in time, before too much damage was done. Once the horny tissue was cut away, a sudden release of foul-smelling grey pus would squirt out – straight into your face, if you weren't careful!

There was a dairy farmer I used to regularly call upon to carry out such tasks on his cows. On one occasion, as I backed the car to drive away, it was neither the cow nor the vet that came to harm, but a hen which had run across my path, and ended up with a neatly fractured leg. The farmer said he would immediately kill the hapless bird, despite me offering to put the injured leg in a plaster, to see if it would heal. 'No, she isn't worth the expense', he protested. But when I said I'd take her home with me, and do it free of charge – except for any eggs she might lay whilst living in my back garden – he agreed the deal with a smile!

With my dear wife's help, Henrietta's leg was duly plastered, and thus she roamed, or rather hopped, around our garden for a good three weeks. She made a lot of mess, but that was all. On the very day I removed the plaster, and checked if all was well before returning her to the farm, she walked across the lawn and left us a parting gift: an egg at last, just to say thank you!

O Jerusalem, Jerusalem, thou that killest the prophets, and stonest them which are sent unto thee, how often would I have gathered thy children together, even as a hen gathereth her chickens under her wings, and ye would not!

Matthew 23:37

FLYING FOX

One morning, I was called out quite early to a sleepy seaside town in North Somerset. The houses and bungalows rested on a ridge sloping down to the sea: a favourite location for retired folk, and their pets. My visit didn't take long, and on my way home for breakfast, I spotted a fox in one of the gardens, behaving very strangely, as if drugged.

I decided to investigate, and finding no-one about, carefully approached the animal, and was able to catch it. For this, one would use a looped pole, placed over the head and around the neck, to hold it at bay until it could be properly and safely confined in a travel-cage. In some countries, even in Europe, it would be very risky to handle a sick fox, as it might be suffering from rabies. One scratch or bite contaminated with its saliva would be enough to pass on the deadly brain virus. Prompt administration of vaccine and serum would then be needed, as within the next few months, once symptoms develop, a very unpleasant death ensues.

I took Mr Reynard home with me, and put him into my garden shed, to see if he might recover. My dear wife, who could always be relied upon to minister kindness to such 'out-of-the-ordinary' patients, provided bread-and-milk to offer to our guest. As soon as I opened the door, however, he desperately flew around the shed, trying to escape, finally squeezing into a gap under the top of my work-bench. With wild fear in his eyes, he looked out at me as if to say: 'I'm utterly terrified of you, and no way am I coming out of here!' So I put his food down on the floor, and left him alone to recover.

This incident reminds me of the times I had to handle semi-wild cats. Dealing with them in a confined space could be quite scary, as they clambered up walls, hung from curtains, and tried in vain to get away. Human wildness, in the face of kindness, may also be experienced, as when George Müller provided for the orphaned children living rough on the streets of nineteenth century Bristol. Without any direct appeals, he looked by faith to God to touch the hearts of many, and thus to provide the means to feed, clothe and educate many hundreds of these poor little souls. He saw to it, that when they finally left his care, they at least had a chance to make their way in the world.

By the end of the day, Mr Reynard recovered from his apparent drunkenness. Probably he'd eaten something in one of the gardens, such as pellets put down to kill slugs. I took him back to the place where I'd found him, and let him go. Off he flew into the night, without so much as a 'thank you'!

And Jesus said unto him, Foxes have holes, and birds of the air have nests; but the Son of man hath not where to lay his head.

Luke 9:58

LOVABLE HOUNDS

Whether it's a Great Dane, a Chihuahua, or something in between, it's still a dog, and will usually be someone's precious companion. Intriguingly, a person's looks or character is often reflected in their dog!

Whenever you go into a vet's waiting room, you'll see normally brave dogs clinging to their owner's knee, quivering, whimpering and panting. It's quite obvious the vet's surgery is the last place on earth they want to be. I love to see the child-like joy and relief on their faces, as they pull their owners out through the door to go home!

In my private practice days, I might examine a dog at the surgery late at night, because during week-days, I looked after farm animals only. I would ask the owner the dog's name, age and (if it wasn't too obvious) its breed. I remember a lady with a strong South African accent bringing her Bassett Hound for attention at about 11.00 o'clock one evening. The animal was placed on the table, and looked up at us with the typical droopy, blood-shot eyes of the breed. 'What's his name?' I asked. With great seriousness, and not a flicker of a smile, she said *'Dubloon'*. With his sad expression, and the curt demeanour of his mistress, I admit I had to suppress an embarrassing giggle! Well, it was late, and there wasn't much wrong with him: she only wanted a last-minute export health certificate.

One meets all sorts of characters in the doggy world. Usually, as I drive into a farmyard, the farm dogs are the welcoming party. Apart from the noisy reception, they invariably see it as their absolute duty to sniff and spray my wheels. Some of the perkiest are Jack Russell Terriers and the like, which love to be involved in everything going. But they can be very perceptive, too: a farmer's widow told me how their little dog, normally 'full of beans', brought comfort to his master by lying quietly on his lap in the last days of his illness.

It's amazing how many roles dogs play in the service of man. There are sheep dogs, cattle dogs, guide-dogs, sniffer dogs, police dogs, hunting dogs, racing dogs, sledge dogs, guard dogs, gun dogs, fun dogs and (dare I say) totally useless dogs! Whenever I had occasion to visit a hunt kennels, I'd see packs of hounds of various types, and even, in one instance, a small pack of wolves, kept in a secure, licensed enclosure. Their owner liked to study them, and they might also feature in films.

Strange to say, I'm not actually a doggy person, but I do have a few lovable canine friends. There's one who visits the allotment gardens, and perhaps because I've always made a fuss of her, she races towards me and rolls over to have her tummy tickled. Then there's dear little Molly, who'll jump onto my lap and greet me like a long-lost friend, whenever I visit her owners – here she is, with her squeaky toy!

A man that hath friends must shew himself friendly: and there is a friend that sticketh closer than a brother.

Proverbs 18:24

CRANKY CATS

There are cats, and cranky cats! I guess, as a kind, they're all a bit cranky, because of their artfully aloof dependence on humans. I find them quite lovable – in small doses! Although there's something very comforting about a purring cat, warmly curled up on one's lap, just you wait: they'll jump down as soon as you even look towards the pantry!

I once watched a pretty little tortoiseshell, following her elderly owner to the bus stop. There, she hid in the bushes till the lady returned a couple of hours later. Cats are normally self-contained, however, not needing to be taken for walks, or have sticks thrown. Whilst their hunting instincts keep rats and mice at bay, a collar with a little bell attached could save many of the lovely song birds that grace our gardens.

Normal cats are one thing (if there is such a thing), and cranky cats are quite another! In my travels, I occasionally come across the latter, and am always amused and intrigued by them in equal measure. There's a quaint little medieval town not far from here, which is just the sort of place you might expect to find such a cat. There's an antique china shop, where every square inch is laden and stacked high with beautiful old crockery. You have to be very careful how you go, as it would be so easy to cause an avalanche. At one of my visits, right there at the back of the shop, in the narrow gangway back to safety, lay a big smoky-grey Persian, quite unperturbed, and definitely not minded to move! To get by, one was obliged to carefully step over the monster: but the consequences of losing one's balance in the manoeuvre didn't bear thinking about. This cat came in each morning, having adopted the shop about a year previously. He lay around quite contentedly, until about ten minutes from closing time, and then strolled out on his way home – wherever that might have been!

Another character lived on a farm I'd visited about four years before. He was 18 years old then, and I was aware this tabby was rather special. At a later visit, I asked the farmer: 'Do you still have that old moggie of yours?' 'Yes', he said, as we entered the cosy kitchen. There he was, lolled out full-stretch on the kitchen table. 'Watch 'e doesn't bite yer', I was warned, as I went to tickle him under his chin. 'I expect you've very few teeth left now old chap', I said. 'Felix' was mildly flattered by my attentions, but as we needed to sit down at the table, his master turfed him off with a good-humoured *'gid-oud-of-it'*. Slightly disgruntled, the old moggie simply moved to his favourite chair, next to the fire. His demeanour told me that at 22, he was still every bit a cranky cat!

First prize, however, must go to another Persian, who was black with a white bib. His owner, who kept several hives of bees and a few emus, as well as cattle and sheep, was as eccentric as his cat! It sat like a fluffy cushion on a stool, about a metre off the ground, eyeing me with cautious disdain. I was warned not to touch him, as he was said to be nasty with his claws. It was then I learned of his claim to fame. 'Watch this!' his owner said, as he walked across the kitchen, and switched on an electric organ. The cat was wont to come alive, run across the room, and alight on the key board, intent on walking up and down to play a tune (of sorts!): except on this occasion he was rather coy in my presence, and refused to perform. Typical: he probably somehow knew I was a vet!

'Buddy', courtesy of 'Memories', Much Wenlock.

All things were made by him; and without him was not any thing made that was made.

John 1:3

MERCY FOR ANIMALS

I've always loved the natural world of the English countryside. And as I've grown older, I cannot bear to see cruelty or unnecessary suffering of any kind. Sadly, in a fallen world, there will always be suffering, but there's a great deal that's unnecessary, and which we can still do something about.

Christ suffered terribly at the hands of sinful men; yet wherever he is preached, the suffering of both man and animals is alleviated. At the height of his earthly ministry, Jesus of Nazareth did good wherever he went. When John the Baptist found himself in prison, he sent word to Jesus, asking: *'Art thou he that should come, or do we look for another?'* Jesus' reply says it all: *'Go and shew John again those things which ye do hear and see: the blind receive their sight, and the lame walk, the lepers are cleansed, and the deaf hear, the dead are raised up, and the poor have the gospel preached to them. And blessed is he, whosoever shall not be offended in me'* (Matthew 11:3-6).

As a foretaste of the glory to come, wherever the Gospel has been proclaimed in the power of the Holy Spirit, the same manifestations have been seen. Broadly speaking, these are confirming signs and wonders, after which the Church settles into a godly life of faith, hope, and charity, awaiting Christ's return. Such fruits saw pagan empires overthrown, societies enlightened, and all civilized virtue established. Justice, compassion, learning, art, music, architecture and many other benefits, grew beside the Gospel's healing waters, and formed the essential foundations of our culture. Parliaments, law courts, universities, schools and hospitals – all had their roots in God's truth. But just as Solomon's kingdom flourished so greatly at first, once their hearts were turned aside from the Source and Giver of life, everything became hollow and began to fail.

After the first temple was dedicated in Jerusalem, the Lord appeared to Solomon by night. He said that, should he send drought and pestilence in judgement: *'If my people, which are called by my name, shall humble themselves, and pray, and seek my face, and turn from their wicked ways; then will I hear from heaven, and will forgive their sin, and will heal their land'* (2 Chronicles 7:14).

In 1904, a great Christian revival broke out in the chapels of South Wales. This powerful move of God spread throughout Wales, and rippled around the world. Some memorable effects are recorded, even in the local newspapers of the day. Despite the fervour of daily prayer meetings, productivity in the mines increased! Pubs closed for lack of business, drunkenness and crime were so scarce that the police cells and courts were empty, and long-standing debts and family feuds were settled. And the poor pit ponies, confused at no longer being cursed, cajoled and goaded as before, were reluctant to work!

That last effect of a holy revival brings tears to my eyes. Oh, that we might see such a time again! Or could it be that the world has now entered that dark period that Jesus warned would come, just prior to his return? For *'The night is far spent; the day is at hand'*!

A righteous man regardeth the life of his beast: but the tender mercies of the wicked are cruel.

Proverbs 12:10

ADVENT HYMN

Joy to the world, the Lord is come!
Let earth receive her King;
Let every heart prepare Him room,
And heav'n and nature sing,
And heav'n and nature sing,
And heav'n, and heav'n, and nature sing.

Joy to the earth, the Saviour reigns!
Let men their songs employ;
While fields and floods, rocks, hills, and plains
Repeat the sounding joy,
Repeat the sounding joy,
Repeat, repeat, the sounding joy.

No more let sins and sorrows grow,
Nor thorns infest the ground;
He comes to make His blessings flow
Far as the curse is found,
Far as the curse is found,
Far as, far as, the curse is found.

He rules the world with truth and grace,
And makes the nations prove
The glories of His righteousness,
And wonders of His love,
And wonders of His love,
And wonders, wonders, of His love.

Isaac Watts 1674-1748

He appointed the moon for seasons: the sun knoweth his going down. Thou makest darkness, and it is night: wherein all the beasts of the forest do creep forth.

Psalm 104:19-20

BEASTS OF BURDEN

The noble creatures that once pulled carts or ploughs, or bore their riders over long distances, have all but vanished from our countryside and towns. In other countries, though, there are still many working horses, donkeys, mules, oxen, buffalo, camels and even elephants!

As a small boy, I used to watch a neighbour walk his magnificent Shire horse out of its stable, down to the edge of the fields. The heavy clip-clop across the road, and the smell of horse and leather on the breeze, is unforgettable. A padded collar would be placed over the horse's head and linked-up with the various pieces of harness, ready for drawing the single-furrow plough, harrow, cart or other tackle. It was a slow, orderly procedure in which the man and his beast skilfully co-operated. By this time, I remember my grandfather was using a small tractor to pull a reaper-binder, but many of these machines up till then had been drawn by a pair of heavy horses. For all the convenience of a tractor, there's no doubt that the loss of that special bond with these magnificent animals was a source of heartache to many.

The milkman, the coal merchant, and the 'Rag-and-Bone' man, were among those still using horses to draw their carts through the streets where I grew-up, even as late as the mid-1950's; but one rarely sees such working horses nowadays. One old farmer told me he didn't regret this, as there was a lot of suffering when horses were over-driven or became lame. In some poorer parts of the world, this is still sadly true. Animals are so often the innocent sharers of human suffering and sorrow, as they were on the battlefield, in cavalry days. Vets are sorely needed in such situations.

John Wesley, the eighteenth-century evangelist, travelled the length and breadth of the land to proclaim the Gospel, and is said to have travelled 4-5,000 miles a year on horseback. He would read and make notes whilst in the saddle, and his journals record occasions when his horse stumbled or became lame. The work was so urgent to Wesley, he would resort to prayer for both himself and his horse, enabling him to complete his arduous journey, and fulfil his mission at a particular place, on time.

How remarkable, that in the world's advanced countries, it's barely 100 years since motor cars, lorries and tractors took over from the noble horse. But horses, along with donkeys, mules, oxen, camels and other beasts of burden are still best suited to some terrains, as they have been for generations. When Abraham's servant was sent back to his master's kindred to find a wife for his precious son, Isaac, young Rebecca was signified as the bride-to-be when she said: *'I will draw water for thy camels also, until they have done drinking'*. Her caring heart for the weary camels led to her becoming the mother of Israel, from whom Messiah himself would one day arise.

Hast thou given the horse strength? hast thou clothed his neck with thunder?

Job 39:19

ANIMAL WAR HEROS

It is a sad fact that our original God-given dominion over the creatures, now subject to the Fall, is seen also in the horrors of war. This is certainly the case for horses, from time immemorial; also for camels; and when Hannibal famously crossed the Alps, even for elephants! Mules were used a great deal in difficult terrain to carry munitions and supplies, and in certain roles, dogs also.

A number of vets I knew had been officers in the Royal Army Veterinary Corps. Founded in 1796, the work of the RAVC played a key role in looking after such animals, even in WW2. Up to and including WW1, horses were used, not only for cavalry, but for drawing gun carriages and transporting supplies and wounded. There was such a shortage of horses that many from the farms were sent to the front, never to be seen again. Many of the men formed bonds of affection with their charges, and did their best to show them kindness amidst the appalling carnage. The British army alone used over a million horses in WW1, with casualties in the hundreds of thousands.

Many dogs were also used, and fulfilled all sorts of useful roles, including advance warning of poison gas attacks. A Bull Terrier known as 'Sergeant Stubby', with the American 102nd Infantry Regiment, was a remarkable example. Thousands of pigeons were used to transfer messages, and all sorts of other bizarre uses for animals were tried. Attempts were even made to train sea lions to detect submarines!

One day, fairly recently, a Polish colleague of mine turned-up at work wearing a T-shirt featuring a bear called 'Wojtek' (pronounced Voytek). I learned that Wojtek was a Polish war hero: a remarkable Syrian bear that had been picked-up as an orphaned cub by Polish soldiers released from internment in Russia, as they made their way down through the Caspian Sea area to join forces with the allies in the Mediterranean. Eventually, the bear was adopted by 22nd Artillery Supply Company of the Polish II Corps, and given the rank of 'Private'. Wojtek loved to wrestle with the soldiers, and learned to carry artillery shells! He took part in the long, fierce battle of Monte Cassino, Italy; such was the affection and admiration of the soldiers for this characterful bear, he was promoted to 'Corporal'. Sadly, at the end of the war, when Polish II Corps was transferred to Scotland and demobilized, Wojtek became redundant and was given to Edinburgh Zoo, where he lived until 1963. It's said he would warm to Polish visitors, being familiar with the language. There's a bronze statue of him in Edinburgh, near the castle: a poignant memorial to a lovable bear, and a lovable and longsuffering people.

And the cow and the bear shall feed; their young ones shall lie down together: and the lion shall eat straw like the ox.

Isaiah 11:7

FLOREAT SALOPIA

'A large and lovely county, generally fair and fruitful, affording grass, grain and all things necessary for man's sustenance': so wrote historian Rev. Thomas Fuller (1608-1661) about Shropshire, in Volume 3 of his *'Worthies of England'*. Having had the privilege of working there for over forty years, I can testify to the accuracy of his description.

The county affords a varied landscape, both hill country and lowlands, and is bounded on the west by Offa's Dyke – a legacy of the 8th century King of Mercia, setting out the then border with Wales. The area had been familiar with conflict since Roman times, and well into the Middle Ages, as witnessed by the many earthworks and fortifications. The remains of the old Roman city of Wroxeter are quite spectacular: Viroconium, as they called it, was once the fourth largest city in Britain, and lies at the end of Watling Street, a Roman road that stretches some 250 miles all the way back to Dover in Kent. But for all its long history, this largest of the inland counties is still quite sparsely populated.

By virtue of the region's upland grazings, including the neighbouring hills of Wales, trading in livestock has been a prominent feature for generations: hence many Shropshire farmers have Welsh surnames. There are at least five distinct terrains within the county, each with its own local accent. The farming community is close-knit, with strong mutual ties and a well-established trade network. Shrewsbury is the central market town, with roads radiating outwards to a number of other market towns, some twenty or so miles distant in all directions. But the county had also featured prominently in the Industrial Revolution, through novel methods of iron-smelting by the Quaker, Abraham Darby, at Coalbrookdale. He made the first Iron Bridge there. And just a short distance away, John Rose made beautiful, world-famous, Coalport china.

It's been a great joy to get to know Shropshire and its people. Even after all this time, I still come across little hamlets or farmsteads I've never been to before. To drive through such beautiful countryside is one thing, but to sit down in the farmhouse and engage with its custodians has been a very special privilege in my latter years.

Notable godly men associated with the county include the Puritan, Richard Baxter, and Wesley's friend, John Fletcher of Madeley. Also, Rev. Thomas Bray, 1658-1730, who from limited means, founded SPG and SPCK: societies which promoted the propagation of the Gospel and Christian knowledge at home and abroad. He established many libraries to support isolated ministers and missionaries, and these were a lifeline in the American colonies, where he took a keen interest in the spiritual welfare of settlers, slaves and Indians alike. He was born at Marton, near Chirbury, hence a plaque to his memory in the Parish Church. I'm sure they'd all agree with me about Shropshire. Yet, also, how dark the world is without the light of Christ! With faithful Abraham, I remember I'm only a sojourner here. Wild white violets in a hedge-bottom at Vernald's Common remind me of the County Motto: *'Floreat Salopia': 'May Shropshire Flourish'*. Rare, pure and unassuming in their simple beauty, they cheer the passing pilgrim on his upward path to the celestial city.

For here have we no continuing city, but we seek one to come.

Hebrews 13:14

THE CATTLE ON A THOUSAND HILLS

I see many wonderful sights in my travels. It may be simply a field of contented, healthy cattle, or a bunch of yearlings looking over a gate, or a clean-fleeced flock of sheep on a hill.

If you farm in the hill country, you cannot grow much by way of crops, because the ground is uneven, the soil poor and shallow, and the weather cooler and wetter. Such terrain is best suited to a pastoral way of life, where the cattle and sheep can roam, and convert the upland pastures into meat and wool. It may be harder to make a living by this means, as much depends on the seasonal sales of weaned calves and lambs to the lowland famers. But the lifestyle, for all its hardships, has its attractions.

By contrast, the lowland farmer is able to grow corn and other crops, as well as raising livestock. The traditional influx of hardy stock from the hills is good for the land, and uses up surplus crops or grass. For example, many hill sheep are brought down to lowland farms in winter, to graze-off the grass left over from the previous season. This is beneficial for both sward and soil; and for a small headage payment, the hill farmer secures good winter keep for his young ewes. On some unfenced hills or mountains, the older breeding ewes stay out, or come down to in-by land. They know their own individual patch of ground, or 'heaf': hence they are called 'hefted' sheep, but are marked to denote their owner. Some may only come off the hill in bad weather, or special gatherings for dipping, shearing and other husbandry tasks.

The dairy farmer pursues a very different lifestyle to the herdsmen of the uplands. His cattle are bred to eat large amounts of lush grass and balanced concentrate rations, to produce, in-turn, large quantities of milk. Apart from delicious butter, cream and cheese, much of the food we eat contains milk in one form or another. The calves are reared as replacements or as beef, especially the beef cross-bred calves. As with all things, man tries to get the edge on his competitors, to be able to produce more and more for less and less. But often such 'progress' leads to problems, such as low prices through over-production, or health issues for the animals. The successful farmer must find a balance to suit his own circumstances and try to keep going, or adapt to other ways of making a living. Life was always hard on the land and is no less so today, with the many pressures these dedicated folk so bravely face.

Jesus said our Father in heaven makes his sun to rise on the evil and the good, and sends rain on the just and the unjust. Yet history shows that Providence was sometimes withheld, as a corrective lesson. Where are we today in this regard, and how far has God's mercy been stretched in our land? How many now even acknowledge or recognize him as the One from whom all blessings flow? Much joy and peace is thus forfeited: yet is so much needed.

For every beast of the forest is mine, and the cattle upon a thousand hills.

Psalm 50:10

GIVE THANKS FOR THE FARMER

One way or another, I've been associated with farming all my life. When I was growing up, it was a relationship tinged with fear: for it was a hard life, which tended to produce hard men! My grandfather was a tenant farmer; and my father worked for another farmer. His employer was also our landlord, as in those days, home ownership or secure tenancies were not generally features of working class life. It's easy to forget how much this affected social customs and outlook, which still lingers-on today.

History and politics are about how we all relate to one another in society as a whole. Look around you, and you'll see what a terrible mess humanity gets into when left to itself. Wars and revolutions erupt like earthquakes, and much suffering is caused on every hand. Sometimes there's a just cause, but without a guiding light, few know what true justice is.

The French Revolution overthrew the rulers of its day. But in Britain, just when the country was at a low moral ebb, a great awakening took place – a revolution of Christian love through the preaching of the Gospel of Christ. The Church of England could not contain it, and it spread outside into the streets and fields. Thousands listened to the anointed preachers. When miners heard the good news of God's mercy through the death of his Son in their place, tears of repentance streamed down their blackened faces. If forgiven by the Almighty at such great cost, how much more the guilty must forgive others!

In the wildest places, in the tiniest hamlets, there are still little chapels, built in those wonderful days following the Wesleyan revival. Although many are now disused, they testify to that great revolution of the past, which was also known by its holy fruits of *'love, joy, peace, longsuffering, gentleness, goodness, faith, meekness, temperance'*, against which there was no law! Such power at work in many converted souls saved Britain from violent revolution. Ordinary men and women worked first for Christ, then for their bosses, and last of all, for themselves. Amidst the darkness, came much peace and blessing, which reached around the world. Elsewhere, in the absence of a Reformation or subsequent revival, the Communists of the 20th century scoffed, and said religion was 'the opium of the masses'. Their godless revolution threw out the old social order, and enslaved or killed millions. And after 70 years, they found it simply didn't work!

Like other men, farmers aren't perfect. But I believe they should be highly honoured and respected. And besides, without them, we should starve! Their skills are passed down through the generations. They work hard, and against many odds. They are sometimes isolated and feel everything is against them. They keep going when others would give up. Even when tragedy strikes, there are all the animals to feed. Their struggle for freedom on the land is also our struggle. No wonder I came to love them!

I exhort therefore, that, first of all, supplications, prayers, intercessions, and giving of thanks, be made for all men; for kings, and for all that are in authority; that we may lead a quiet and peaceable life in all godliness and honesty. For this is good and acceptable in the sight of God our Saviour; who will have all men to be saved, and to come unto the knowledge of the truth. For there is one God, and one mediator between God and men, the man Christ Jesus; who gave himself a ransom for all, to be testified in due time.

1 Timothy 2:1-6

A FARMER'S HYMN

We plough the fields, and scatter
The good seed on the land,
But it is fed and watered
By God's Almighty hand;
He sends the snow in winter,
The warmth to swell the grain,
The breezes and the sunshine,
And soft refreshing rain.

All good gifts around us
Are sent from heaven above;
Then thank the Lord, O thank the Lord,
For all His love.

He only is the Maker
Of all things near and far;
He paints the wayside flower,
He lights the evening star;
The winds and waves obey Him,
By Him the birds are fed;
Much more to us His children,
He gives our daily bread.

We thank Thee then, O Father,
For all things bright and good,
The seed-time and the harvest,
Our life, our health, our food;
Accept the gifts we offer
For all Thy love imparts,
And, what Thou most desirest,
Our humble, thankful hearts.
                              Amen.

Matthias Claudius, 1740-1815;
Translated by Jane Montgomery Campbell, 1817-78

Thou visitest the earth, and waterest it: thou greatly enrichest it with the river of God, which is full of water: thou preparest them corn, when thou hast so provided for it. Thou waterest the ridges thereof abundantly: thou settlest the furrows thereof: thou makest it soft with showers: thou blessest the springing thereof. Thou crownest the year with thy goodness; and thy paths drop fatness. They drop upon the pastures of the wilderness: and the little hills rejoice on every side. The pastures are clothed with flocks; the valleys also are covered over with corn; they shout for joy, they also sing.

Psalm 65:9-13

A COW CALLED PATCH

One day I had to visit a widow who lived in a little upland village, surrounded by her animals and poultry. For the first time ever, her beef breeding herd had been hit by the scourge of tuberculosis. It was quite a shock, when out of a herd of only thirty or so, six cows had reacted to the annual skin test. My role was to try to establish how this notifiable infection got into the herd, and to advise on how to cut down the risk in future. Reactor herds are subject to movement restrictions, so the farmer is unable to buy or sell cattle as usual. Once the risk has lessened, a licence may be issued to allow limited trading, until such time as the herd has finally tested clear on two successive occasions, sixty days apart.

This remarkable lady, then in her late seventies, somehow continued to cope despite minimal help. Apart from the cattle, she also had some very nice pigs, an assorted collection of poultry of every description, and the usual dogs and cats. One of the great pleasures of this phase of my career was meeting and giving moral support to so many farmers, of which no two were alike. I had a great love for them all, because of their tenacity and dedication to their livestock, even when everything seemed against them. Anyone who loves and cares for animals will know how hard it is to lose them, especially when it is due to factors largely beyond their control.

As is so often the case, a characterful owner attracts characterful animals! A hen wandered into the kitchen, where she'd been known to fly up onto a windowsill to lay an egg. There was an 18-year old bull called Jonathan, of a breed not known for its quietness. But in this case, he'd placidly allow each foot to be placed in turn on a wooden block, for his hooves to be trimmed-up!

Before leaving, I was asked to look at a lovely old cow called 'Patch'. She was one of the six Tb-reactors, but had been allowed to stay on the farm a few days longer, until she'd calved. We walked up a steep track to a small isolated paddock where she was grazing, her beautiful new-born calf lying down nearby. It was a sunny afternoon in May, and as I pondered the idyllic scene, I was struck by the tragedy of it all. Within a day or two, 'Patch' was to go, leaving her baby behind to be reared on the bucket.

Normally, the Tb is found in certain small lymph glands only, so once passed at inspection, the rest of the meat is safe to eat. Occasionally, if the animal has had recent treatment with medicines, or cannot travel due to lameness or some other ailment, compensation is still payable, but the meat is not salvaged. In this instance, there was risk of injury to the very large milky udder, and the owner was concerned for Patch's welfare, right through to her journey's end. I therefore gave permission for the cow to be put down on-farm by the local knacker man. Usually, I never saw the many cattle that had to go under these compulsory terms, but on this occasion, the full impact of the loss came home to me.

He causeth the grass to grow for the cattle, and herb for the service of man: that he may bring forth food out of the earth;

Psalm 104:14

BADGER BLUES

There was a wood near a famous film studio, where many a notable scene had been shot. Certain of us keen young naturalists at school found a badger sett there, and we'd hide downwind just before dusk, to watch Act II of Earth's daily drama unfold.

The birds would quieten in their roosts, as an eerie hush settled upon the scene. As the creatures of the night began to stir, and as we sat quiet and still, we'd hear little rustlings: perhaps of a stag beetle or a shrew among the dry leaves; or the hoot of an owl; or the whine of mosquitos about our heads. Before long, the 'badger folk' peered out from their burrows, cautiously sniffing the cool night air. By and by, we'd see their shadowy moonlit forms, as they scratched and played, and shuffled off into the woods and pastures beyond.

The first port of call would be their latrines, a series of shallow hollows in the soil. I'd take samples of the droppings back to the biology lab next day, and wash them through a series of sieves to find clues as to the badger diet: remnants of beech-mast or acorns, or the occasional undigested body parts of a beetle or wasp. We knew they also loved earthworms and anything sweet or starchy. Badgers were not very common then, so were definitely worthy of an article in the school magazine. Little did I know the tragic role badgers would come to play in my work, many years later.

Most of my professional life I've been actively involved in government efforts to eradicate tuberculosis from cattle. This was important because bovine Tb could also infect humans, especially in the days before milk was heat treated ('pasteurised'), and before there were any effective antibiotics. Many little children suffered fatal illness from Tb in those pre-WW2 days, including one of my mother's sisters, who died from it as a one-year old baby.

Pasteurisation of milk, and the post-war campaign to eradicate Tb from cattle, meant that human Tb from this source was now almost unheard of. Great strides were made until the early 1970's, when it was realized a wildlife reservoir in certain areas of the West Country was hindering the spectacular progress made elsewhere. It was discovered that among all the wildlife species, the badger was especially prone to infection with the same bacterium that causes Tb in cattle. The culling of badgers in those areas, mainly by gassing, soon led to a dramatic improvement, and it looked as if the country was at last rapidly on course to be rid of the disease from both cattle and wildlife for good.

But many people began to feel sorry for the badger, and campaigned to limit or stop the culling. They seemed not to think of the impact on the farmer, his livestock, other wildlife or even the badger itself. Eventually, protection under the law meant that badgers became very common, and in the absence of an effective vaccine, Tb continued to spread to cattle further afield, even into large areas of the country from whence it had once been eradicated. As fast as the infected cattle were removed, others could catch the disease from the openly infected badgers foraging in their pastures and byres – an outcome that has since caused great suffering and loss to both man and animals.

Be thou diligent to know the state of thy flocks, and look well to thy herds. For riches are not for ever: and doth the crown endure to every generation?

Proverbs 27:23-24

PERKY PIG

Farms and their owners vary greatly. Some are small one-man-bands; others are huge businesses with very large numbers of livestock. However, many farms in the areas where I have been privileged to work are medium-sized family enterprises, where survival is everything and failure or selling-up is unthinkable. Some of these farms have seen better days, but are now struggling to cope, with failing health and finances adding to the problems.

When a farmer is left alone, having lost both parents, and there's no wife to give support, isolation and loneliness might mean that both he and his livestock will be at risk. One sometimes sees tremendous tenacity and courage, even when the odds are stacked against them. Although it fell to me to speak-up for the livestock, I also found it essential to try to help the farmer sort himself out, too. The kind help of neighbouring farmers and friends in this regard was always crucial.

Amidst the muddling along, one might see all sorts of strange sights. As a result of cattle and pigs being housed together in a large shed, I once saw a pig helping itself to milk direct from the cow! Ramshackle as such farms may be, the animals try to make the best of things. Provided they have freedom to find adequate food, pigs may sometimes be happier than in a sterile, modern, highly automated set-up. From their point of view, the best home is somewhere between the two, with lots of straw to root around and lie in, which is more difficult to achieve when large numbers are involved.

I remember one such characterful animal, a boar purchased from a local market for fattening. From his rather attractive ginger and black markings, he might have been a Tamworth crossed with a Gloucester Old Spot, but he was certainly distinguished in other ways! He'd break out from the shed where most of the other pigs were housed, and wander around the farm at leisure. He'd root around the paddocks with his snout, as pigs love to do, before taking up residence in his 'penthouse flat'. This was an old hay loft, which he'd access by clambering up the straw-bales in an adjoining barn. From there he'd look out on the world in great comfort: possibly the happiest pig you could find anywhere! It was good while it lasted…

If ye fulfil the royal law according to the scripture, Thou shalt love thy neighbour as thyself, ye do well:

James 2:8

ANIMALS OF THE WIDER WORLD

What an amazing variety of animals we see at the zoo! It would be hard to imagine so many strange and wonderful creatures, if we'd never seen any of them before: the majestic lion, the mighty elephant, the elegant giraffe, the dazzling zebra, and so many other magnificent creatures: the gorilla, the rhinoceros, the hippopotamus, the wildebeest and the antelope. Although they are all so different, they all have two eyes, two ears, four limbs and warm, red blood. Look inside their bodies, and the same general pattern is seen there, too. For any veterinary surgeon who has to deal with them, this is just as well!

Even so, the treatment of exotic animals is a very specialized field. As with all animals, the vet has first to take note of the owner's story, and to closely observe his patient's behaviour, before carrying out a clinical examination and any necessary treatment. With the more dangerous wild animals, the 'hands-on' aspects will usually involve restraint inside a narrow cage with trap-doors, or drugging with a dart, or both. One never takes unnecessary risks with any kind of animal: even the domesticated kind do not like vets!

I remember, during my training, going to see a young elephant at a Circus. Working elephants are really quite tame compared to those in the wild, and with a little help from their keeper, are fairly easy to deal with, especially when young. In this case, our patient was off-food and generally sorry for himself. It was quite a puzzle to work out exactly what was wrong with him. But with his body temperature a little lower than normal, infections could be ruled out, and it seemed most likely he had indigestion from eating too much of something!

Such cases in herbivores often respond to treatment with injections of large doses of vitamin B, given by intravenous injection. This is certainly the case with ruminants such as cattle, when they gorge themselves on too many apples or any form of highly fermentable food, leading to intoxication. But for animals like our baby elephant that were simply off-colour, the injection of a beautiful pink solution of Vitamin B^{12} made everyone feel better!

Many people now feel that circus elephants are made to perform pointless tricks using harsh training methods. These intelligent and lovable animals have had a raw deal in many ways, particularly from the trade in ivory, for which they are often illegally killed, just for their tusks. Indian elephants were used in warfare in the ancient world, and for logging work in the jungles of Southern Asia. It is a comfort to know that one day, God will restore the whole Creation to its former glory. Thy kingdom come, Lord!

And out of the ground the LORD God formed every beast of the field, and every fowl of the air; and brought them unto Adam to see what he would call them: and whatsoever Adam called every living creature, that was the name thereof.

Genesis 2:19.

ANIMALS OF THE DEEP

Earth's rivers and seas teem with life. The mighty Blue Whale, the largest of all Earth's creatures, feeds on swarms of little shrimps called 'krill', which in turn feed on minute algae, called diatoms.

There's a beautiful story of a fisherman who spotted a whale in big trouble out at sea. Entangled and weighed down in a mass of nets and ropes, it was in danger of drowning (remember, every so often, whales have to come up for air). A rescue team decided the only way to free it was to risk diving in alongside to cut it free, which took several hours. Afterwards, the whale swam around in circles, coming back to each diver in turn, gently nudging them, as if to say 'thank you'. Those divers were very deeply moved by this awesome experience!

Only in recent centuries have whales been hunted on a large scale, but this had to stop, to protect them from extinction. Whales and dolphins are quite intelligent, and seem less fearful of man than land animals. In their case, the kinship of dominion that existed in Eden seems to have persisted.

There was a Hebrew prophet called Jonah (Jonas in Greek), who lived in northern Israel in the 8th century BC. He was called to go to Nineveh in ancient Assyria (near Mosul, in modern-day Iraq), a very great city of some 120,000 souls, that could not *discern between their right hand and their left hand; and also much cattle'*. (Yes, God cared for them, too! Jonah 4:11) However, Jonah despised the Ninevites, as the Assyrians had been arch-enemies of Israel. So he boarded a ship bound for faraway Tarshish, thinking to escape the urgent call that was upon him. Once at sea, however, the ship ran into a violent storm, and the heathen sailors cast lots to see who it was that had brought this jinx upon them. The remedy was to throw whoever it was over-board, so that the storm might be calmed: and of course, we might guess who it turned out to be!

The Lord appointed 'a great fish' to swallow Jonah, who spent three days inside it before being vomited up onto dry land. We don't really know what kind of a creature this was, but interestingly, Sperm Whales are known to undertake prolonged dives in search of large squid, so might easily swallow a man whole. They have four stomachs, the first of which is a holding chamber. Moreover, they are known to 'vomit' a waxy substance called 'ambergris', which has been prized for use in perfumery since ancient times.

After this terrifying experience, Jonah realized he couldn't escape God's commission, so he now went to Nineveh, as originally commanded. To his surprise, the Ninevites listened, and humbled themselves before God; so the doom they had faced was, at that time, averted.

Centuries later, the Jews under Roman occupation, despite all the miracles they'd seen, asked Jesus for a sign to prove that he was indeed the promised Messiah. He replied: *'An evil and adulterous generation seeketh after a sign; and there shall no sign be given to it, but the sign of the prophet Jonas: for as Jonas was three days and three nights in the whale's belly; so shall the Son of man be three days and three nights in the heart of the earth'* (Matthew 12:39). Taking account of the timing of Passover that year, this was literally fulfilled.

And God created great whales, and every living creature that moveth, which the waters brought forth abundantly, after their kind, and every winged fowl after his kind: and God saw that it was good.

Genesis 1:21

PENGUINS

I once had to attend a training course to prepare for duties in poultry-meat hygiene. This was to supplement my expertise in red-meat hygiene and humane slaughter regulations. My duties took me to many factories around the country, and on one occasion abroad, to what was then Communist Romania.

A young woman from a top university came to give us a fascinating lecture on avian anatomy, in which she explained to us the amazing variety and bodily design within the bird kingdom. For example, birds have a remarkable respiratory system, featuring air-sacs throughout their bodies, and extending even into their bones. The air they breathe passes to the air sacs and back again via the lungs, thus increasing oxygen absorption, which is so necessary to energise flight. In most birds, the bones themselves are honeycombed, to make them even lighter for flight.

But penguins, being flightless marine birds, had features suited to swimming, and life along the icy Antarctic coasts of the Southern Oceans. In their case, the bones are solid, as they have to overcome buoyancy during diving under water to considerable depths for several minutes at a time. They also have special glands around their beaks, which allow them to drink sea water, and to get rid of the salt! Our lecturer explained all these wonderful features in evolutionary terms, namely that the birds had been kitted-out for their unusual lifestyle through gradual, chance modifications over millions of years.

Such was the wonder of her subject, I felt I had to challenge the evolutionary explanation. Quoting a recent article in a quality newspaper that dared to question Darwinism, I said the wonderful features she'd described were impossible to explain except by Special Creation. My sense of awe in terms of the 'unsayable' was met with an embarrassed silence from the audience, and our lecturer politely responded that she had merely followed the academic convention.

At the end of the session, I went up to the front to have a few private words with her. She looked thoughtfully out of the window for a few moments, then said, that as someone who'd been brought up in a 'Low-Church' (evangelical) background, she was well acquainted with my views. I wonder now if perhaps her enthusiasm for the subject revealed something of a deeper conviction: one that she was not prepared to own at that moment.

The true spirit of scientific enquiry is embodied in the inscription above the doors of the Cavendish Physics Laboratory in Cambridge: *'The works of the Lord are great, sought out of all them that have pleasure therein'* (Psalm 111:2). But whatever clever academics and the 'politically correct' media constantly and so one-sidedly force upon us, there's an all-powerful Creator and Judge to whom we are all ultimately accountable.

And there's but one Name given under heaven, who can speak up for us on Judgement Day – the man, Christ Jesus!

And even as they did not like to retain God in their knowledge, God gave them over to a reprobate mind, to do those things which are not convenient;

Romans 1:28

ANIMALS DOWN UNDER

How strange the animals of the world 'down-under' must have seemed to the first Europeans. Weirdly distinctive, the animals of Australasia are fascinating!

Although warm-blooded and nurturing their young on milk, the majority of these mammals give birth to tiny under-developed babies, which crawl from the birth canal into a pouch on the front of the mother's body: here, they latch onto a teat and continue to grow and take refuge for up to a year. Diverse in form and lifestyle, they range from small mouse-like creatures, to koalas, possums, the monkey-like cuscus, the cat-like quoll, the carnivorous Tasmanian Devil (like a small bear), the recently extinct Tasmanian Tiger (a striped wolf-like animal), and of course, wallabies and kangaroos: all of them remarkably parallel eco-forms to their Old-World counterparts.

But there are even weirder kinds of mammals down there, called Monotremes: the duck-billed platypus and the spiny ant-eater! These lay soft-shelled eggs, incubate them in a pouch, and once hatched, finish them on milk. They have other peculiarities, too. For example, they have a bird-like beak, equipped with electrical sensors to detect their prey, namely, either shrimps and worms, or ants and termites.

Of the 334 species of marsupials known in the world today, 70% live in Australia, Tasmania and New Guinea. The rest live in South America, although there are a few in Central America, and one, the Opossum, in North America. South America and Australasia were probably, not that long ago, connected through Antarctica. And although, for some wise reason, none of these strange creatures now lives in the 'Old World', there's fossil evidence they once did. From a biblical perspective, not only must God have created them all: their original representative types or 'kinds' must have been on the Ark during the Flood. Their final distribution could have been established whilst there were still land bridges, or through rafting on mats of uprooted vegetation.

In God's light, we see light. The placental mammal type of Eurasia matched the redemptive narrative revealed through Israel. In identifying with mankind, Christ was born of a virgin, herself subject to the consequences of the Fall (*'In sorrow shalt thou bring forth children'*). Prophetically, he was the Seed of the woman, the only begotten (firstborn) Son of God, the Passover Lamb: the 'Second Adam', who, with the Father and the Holy Spirit, was the Creator and Redeemer of all!

And it came to pass, as he spake these things, a certain woman of the company lifted up her voice, and said unto him, Blessed is the womb that bare thee, and the paps which thou hast sucked. But he said, Yea rather, blessed are they that hear the word of God, and keep it.

Luke 11:27-28

ANIMALS OF THE PAST

As we see from the fossilized remains of living things in the ground beneath our feet, there was once a world that was very different from the one we know today. A fossil is the outline or skeleton of a long-dead creature that has become preserved in mineral form in the rocks of the earth. However, some dinosaur fossils have been found with soft tissues and DNA still within them, indicating they cannot be millions of years old. There are also many historic pictures and carvings of dinosaurs, indicating that they have been around until quite recently.

Whatever happened, there must have been special conditions for such vast numbers of fossils to have been formed on such a wide scale. Today, things that die are scavenged by other creatures or soon decompose. Also, fossils of sea shells, corals and fish are often found far above today's sea level, or hundreds of miles from the coast, and fossils of tropical creatures are sometimes found in the cold Polar regions. Fossil tree trunks have been found standing upright through many layers of rock, and there are zig-zag coal seams, suggesting a sudden world-wide catastrophe, rather than a gradual build-up of sediment.

If you saw the skeleton of a famous person, how much would it really tell you about their living appearance, mannerisms and character? Although many kinds of animals in that by-gone world were much larger, I doubt we should think of them all as fearsome. There were all kinds of other creatures, too, many of which looked much the same as today, as specimens preserved in amber show.

Originally, everything had been created 'very good', and even after The Fall, mankind lived to great ages. It seems there was one large continent, with low hills, surrounded by warm, shallow seas; and the ground was watered by springs, rather than rain. From the beginning, the redemption of mankind through faith had been in the purposes of God. But such was the eventual corruption and violence of those days, in the words of the Apostle Peter, *'the world that then was, being overflowed with water, perished'*. He prophesied that these things would be scoffed at *'in the last days'*, and Jesus warns such days of judgement will return, albeit in the form of fire (2 Peter 3:2-6; Luke 17:26).

But Noah and his household 'found grace in the eyes of the Lord'. He was directed to build a huge ship, to which breeding pairs of all the land-dwelling animals and birds of that time would be drawn by God, to be preserved. Many ancient cultures, as well as the testimony of Jesus and his apostles, bear witness to the reality of the Genesis Flood. When it finally came, not only was there a deluge from above, but 'the fountains of the great deep' were opened: volcanos and mountains were heaved-up, so that many fossils were left high and dry among vast hills of water-borne sediment. Do we not everywhere see evidence in the rocks of this great catastrophe?

Afterwards, God promised that from then on, there'd be seasons of seedtime and harvest (which might suggest the earth's axis had been tilted). He also affirmed that henceforth, animals could be killed for food, and would become more fearful of Man. And as the earth was now watered by rain, he ordained the sign of the rainbow, as a perpetual promise that the earth would never again be destroyed by a flood. These colossal upheavals appear to have included a seismic division of the earth to form the continents, followed by a northern Ice Age. After this, the post-Flood world would have settled to the many varied terrains and climates we see today, with a rapid, genetically 'downhill' adaptive radiation of plant and animal diversity.

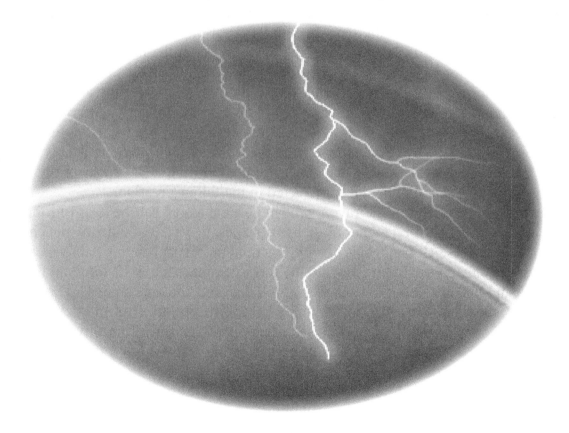

And it shall come to pass, when I bring a cloud over the earth, that the bow shall be seen in the cloud: and I will remember my covenant, which is between me and you and every living creature of all flesh; and the waters shall no more become a flood to destroy all flesh.

Genesis 9:14-15

CLEVER CROW

There's a large horse chestnut tree near my garden, where a family of crows lives. They're very 'talkative', and keep a sharp look-out for intruders. Occasionally, a buzzard soars nonchalantly across the sky, and with loud cries of indignation, the crows send out two or three of their 'fighter planes' to intercept the enemy. They fly rapidly and in a straight line (as crows do) towards the buzzard, an altogether bigger and fiercer bird: and in a spectacular display of aerobatics, dive-bomb it into retreat!

One of these crows had a club foot, its claws curled around like an arthritic hand. He made up for his handicap through cunning, and would bring pieces of hard, stale bread or toast to soak in our bird-bath. One day, he left a fat-ball net, of the type that people hang out for smaller birds. Having found he couldn't get at the fat, he thought he'd try leaving it to soak for a bit – quite clever, really.

The Crow family: Ravens, Crows, Rooks, Jackdaws, Magpies and Jays, are characterful and intelligent birds. Among their tricks are mimicry and the collection of bright objects. They've even been known to return lost items of jewellery, in return for food. Boys would keep baby jackdaws as pets, and train them to say their name – usually simply, *'Jack'*! But they also steal the eggs and chicks of other birds, and have other nasty habits. The mystery of good and ill is indeed reflected in the fallen Creation.

Mr Crow's larger cousin, the raven, whose guttural voice can be heard in the wild places near here, gets several mentions in the Bible. His ways have evidently not changed at all for generations. Although he's not without honour, his scavenging habits mean he's seen as an 'unclean' bird. The raven and the dove were the first to be released from the Ark by Noah after the Flood, to see whether the dry land had appeared. The raven went to and fro, and no doubt rested by perching on top of the ark. But the delicate dove returned to Noah within, until a week later, she came back with an olive leaf (some trees and plants had probably survived as great floating rafts). After a further week had passed, she was able to return to the wild.

When the prophet Elijah took refuge by a brook in the wilderness in the midst of famine, God appointed the ravens to bring him food. But in the end, John's Revelation speaks of Babylon, the world's false religious system, as *'the habitation of devils, and the hold of every foul spirit, and a cage of every unclean and hateful bird'* (18:2). Will you be as a wild, unclean raven, or as a gentle harmless dove? As Noah put forth his hand and pulled the dove in to him, so Christ will graciously welcome those who fly to him for refuge and rest.

Consider the ravens: for they neither sow nor reap; which neither have storehouse nor barn; and God feedeth them: how much more are ye better than the fowls?

Luke 12:24

ANIMALS OF THE BIBLE

Every living thing that was ever created is encompassed in Holy Scripture – and every other created thing as well, including the stars! But as the sixty-six books that make up the Bible are written almost entirely by a people chosen by God to be the custodians of his saving purpose, the animals that feature the most, relate to the ancient pastoral lifestyle of the Hebrews.

The next thing to note is the symbolism of biblical animals. There are animals and birds which are 'clean', and those which are 'unclean'. There are animals that represent submission and innocence, and those that represent evil, rebellion and guile. This does not mean that the animals themselves are good or bad: except, that is, when it comes to eating them for food. In those days, especially, it was generally not a good idea, health-wise, to eat animals that scavenge, or feed on the flesh of other animals.

Right from the start, the humble sheep is centre-stage, less so the wilful goat or the powerful ox. In the beginning, God had blessed Adam and Eve saying, *'Be fruitful, and multiply, and replenish the earth, and subdue it'*, and they were to have dominion over all the creatures. But after the spiritual corruption of the Fall, and their banishment from the Paradise of Eden, God clothed them in animal skins, implying the killing of the innocent to provide a covering for the guilty. The theme continues with Abel's offering of a lamb; then the provision of a young ram lamb caught in a thicket, as a substitute for Abraham's long-promised son, Isaac; later, the 'Passover' lamb, killed for each household upon leaving Egypt; and on into Roman times, John the Baptist points to Jesus of Nazareth, saying: *'Behold the Lamb of God!'* And finally, the Apostle John, caught up to heaven, sees *'the Lamb slain from the foundation of the world'*.

Sin is a most terrible thing, of which we are all guilty before a holy God; and without the shedding of atoning blood, there's no escape from its eternal consequences. But where sin abounded, grace abounded more so! As with Isaac, a substitute was offered in our place, so that whoever believes in him will not perish, but have everlasting life. *'Love so amazing, so divine, demands my soul, my life, my all'*!

Some will argue this shows the Bible speaks only figuratively. On the contrary, all was so literally and historically fulfilled in Christ, exactly as foretold by the prophets over long ages. He literally became *'a sign destined to be rejected'* by his very own people, which shows the whole account from Genesis to Revelation is both divinely inspired and manifestly true. More amazing still, this rejection led to the Gospel being taken to all the nations, until such time as God would turn again to deliver his beloved ancient people. *'The Lion of the Tribe of Judah'*, having laid hold-of and bound *'the dragon, that old serpent'*, will come to deliver them, and reign at last as their true and rightful Messiah-King.

   The Lamb was powerfully anointed by the Spirit in the form of a gentle *dove*; his final journey into Jerusalem was on a lowly *donkey*. But on the day of his return, he will be seated upon a white *war-horse*!

Behold the Lamb of God, which taketh away the sin of the world.

John 1:29b

A GOSPEL HYMN

And can it be that I should gain
An interest in the Saviour's blood?
Died He for me, who caused His pain—
For me, who Him to death pursued?
Amazing love! How can it be,
That Thou, my God, shouldst die for me?

'Tis mystery all: th'Immortal dies:
Who can explore His strange design?
In vain the firstborn seraph tries
To sound the depths of love divine.
'Tis mercy all! Let earth adore,
Let angel minds inquire no more.

He left His Father's throne above
So free, so infinite His grace—
Emptied Himself of all but love,
And bled for Adam's helpless race:
'Tis mercy all, immense and free,
For O my God, it found out me!

Long my imprisoned spirit lay,
Fast bound in sin and nature's night;
Thine eye diffused a quickening ray—
I woke, the dungeon flamed with light;
My chains fell off, my heart was free,
I rose, went forth, and followed Thee.

Still the small inward voice I hear,
That whispers all my sins forgiven;
Still the atoning blood is near,
That quenched the wrath of hostile Heaven.
I feel the life His wounds impart;
I feel the Saviour in my heart.

No condemnation now I dread;
Jesus, and all in Him, is mine;
Alive in Him, my living Head,
And clothed in righteousness divine,
Bold I approach th'eternal throne,
And claim the crown, through Christ my own.

Charles Wesley 1707-88

There is therefore now no condemnation to them which are in Christ Jesus

Romans 8:1a

A HYMN OF PRAISE

O For a thousand tongues to sing
My great Redeemer's praise!
The glories of my God and King,
The triumphs of His grace!

My gracious Master and my God,
Assist me to proclaim,
To spread through all the world abroad
The honours of Thy name.

Jesus! the Name that charms our fears,
That bids our sorrows cease;
'Tis music in the sinner's ears,
'Tis life, and health, and peace.

He breaks the power of cancelled sin,
He sets the prisoner free;
His blood can make the foulest clean,
His blood availed for me.

He speaks, and, listening to his voice,
New life the dead receive;
The mournful, broken hearts rejoice;
The humble poor believe.

Hear him, ye deaf; his praise, ye dumb,
Your loosened tongues employ;
Ye blind, behold your Saviour come,
And leap, ye lame, for joy!

Look unto him, ye nations; own
Your God, ye fallen race;
Look, and be saved through faith alone,
Be justified by grace.

See all your sins on Jesus laid;
The Lamb of God was slain;
His soul was once an offering made
For every soul of man.

Charles Wesley 1707-88

The author in his element: December 2009

I will sing, yea, I will sing praises unto the LORD

Psalm 27:6b

THE BLACKBIRD STILL SINGS

How beautiful is the song of the Blackbird in Spring, bringing joy, tinged with sadness: his pure golden notes echo the bitter-sweetness in the lives of all living things, yet inspire also a glorious hope.

In my dealings with the people of the countryside, I see the exact image of these things: a life of toil tinged with sadness, yet borne up by hope. I have often seen bereavement and loss, yet with a purposeful resolve, they know that they must pick themselves up and carry on. And when they simply cannot, other kind souls draw alongside to help, or to say 'rest awhile', whilst we feed and tend the animals and fields, and sort out a score of other pressing things. These noble fellow-sufferers understand each other's trials, and might well think to themselves as they awake on a spring morning, or after a night in the lambing shed: 'Well, the Blackbird still sings!'

But there's a deeper message here, and one which I feel I must bring. Could there come a time when the Blackbird will *not* sing? And if so, has this happened before in history? Israel, in ancient times was the chosen beacon of the true and only God, the Creator of all, with whom they were (and are still) in an everlasting covenant. There came a time when their falling-away from that light became so grievous, that God could no longer delight in them. After repeated warnings, judgement in the form of famine, pestilence, sword and exile came upon them. The land which had once flowed with milk and honey now mourned. Such is the wilful hardness and blindness of fallen humanity, even when the light of the truth has been freely known in a nation, it may be taken from them and hidden from their eyes. In the calamity that eventually follows, *'evil men understand not judgement, but they that seek the Lord understand all things'* (Proverbs 28:5).

Around the 1550s, some three hundred of our countrymen from every walk of life (including women and youths, two of whom were blind girls), paid with their lives for the true Gospel of Christ, as brought to light in the Reformation. One of them, Bishop Latimer, cried out to another, Nicholas Ridley, as they were about to be burned at the stake as heretics at Oxford: *'Be of good comfort, Master Ridley, and play the man! We shall this day light such a candle, by God's grace, in England, as I trust shall never be put out!'* It is wonderful to think that the light from that candle has since spread across the world.

So what can we do about all these things? It's very clearly laid out for us in the Bible, especially in the words of Jesus and his apostles: and it starts with you and me. In living by faith in the grace of Christ as God intended, we shall be as salt and light in the world. Salt preserves from decay, and light dispels darkness: until such time as Jesus returns to deal with all that is wrong, and to bring in everlasting righteousness.

For the mountains will I take up a weeping and wailing, and for the habitations of the wilderness a lamentation, because they are burned up, so that none can pass through them; neither can men hear the voice of the cattle; both the fowl of the heavens and the beast are fled; they are gone.

Jeremiah 9:10

ANIMAL PLAGUES

During Queen Victoria's reign, as international trade in animals and animal products increased, governments set up veterinary services to stamp-out and control animal diseases that could spread rapidly, destroy livelihoods or even cause famine. Some of these animal diseases could also infect humans: for example, Tuberculosis, Anthrax, Rabies and Bird 'Flu'. Anyone suspecting them had to notify the authorities immediately, so that powers enacted by Parliament could be mobilized. This might mean humanely killing the affected and exposed livestock, and paying compensation to the owner.

In the years 1865-67, Britain was badly hit by 'Rinderpest' or 'Cattle Plague', which was believed to have arrived in live cattle imported from Europe. Whole herds were very rapidly wiped out, as the virus spread from farm to farm. This catastrophic event is commemorated on cattle grave stones, not far from here.

In a tract entitled *'The Finger of God'*, faithful divine, Bishop J C Ryle, vividly described the plague's impact: *'It is a wide-spread calamity. There is hardly a county in England which is not suffering. There is not a family which will not sooner or later suffer. The meat on the rich man's table, and the cheese in the cottage, the milk and butter which form so large a portion of our food, all will be affected by it. It will reach every home, and come home to all.'* Having cited among the sins of the nation, a growing infidelity towards God, covetousness and immorality, he continued: *'Let politicians make the best laws they can to meet the present emergency. Let medical men* (vets) *use every possible means to arrest the plague, and patiently try every remedy. Let practical agriculturists neglect nothing that may be available to prevent contagion, to diminish the liability to infection, and to stamp out the plague when it arises. But my standpoint is that of the Bible. In the light of that book, I raise my concluding question: What shall we all do?'*

Queen Victoria called a National Day of Prayer, for a humbling before God, and to ask for Divine Mercy, to stop the tide of death: which in due course, it was. Much later, vaccines were developed, and by the early 21st Century, the virus finally became extinct worldwide. However, many other nasty animal plagues are still at large today, with which government vets are constantly at war!

Also at this time, another unpleasant virus was affecting our cattle, sheep and pigs: namely, Foot and Mouth Disease (FMD), as it has periodically, ever since. This doesn't kill the livestock, but makes them unthrifty, hindering trade. A very serious FMD epidemic occurred in Britain in 2001, resulting in millions of animals being killed, and a huge financial loss to the country.

Do all these calamities, indeed, have a spiritual root-cause? The effects of sin are real, both in this present age, and eternally. No-one could be more loving and able to heal and bless mankind than Christ: yet it was he who said that in the days just before his return, there'd be earthquakes, wars, famines and pestilences, worldwide. Love for the creatures and our fellow men mean we must always try to make things better; but we also need to pray for God's help, and for that glorious day when Christ returns, when all such horrors will finally be past: *'Thy Kingdom come, Lord, thy will be done in earth, as it is in heaven!*

THIS STONE
IS RAISED AS A
MEMENTO OF
THE GREAT CATTLE
PLAGUE OF 1866, WHICH
SWEPT 54 HEAD OFF
THIS FARM IN 14 DAYS
IN MARCH.
THEY DIED WITHOUT
REMEDY AND HERE LIE

"Shall we receive good from God, and not evil?"

Job 2.10

Personal photograph, by kind permission of Mr & Mrs Heath

Offer unto God thanksgiving; and pay thy vows unto the most High: and call upon me in the day of trouble: I will deliver thee, and thou shalt glorify me.
Psalm 50:14-15

A NEW KIND OF PLAGUE

The 1980s were marked by a wave of problems to do with the wholesomeness of the food we eat. It is of course understandable that farmers try to remain ahead, but it seems that the materialism of the age led everyone astray. Advances in technology had made it possible for all sorts of new ideas to be tried, with a view to producing cheaper food to 'feed the world'. But whilst many in third-world countries continued to starve, Western countries were falling foul of natural boundaries, which, as nations that have had access to the revealed Word of God for generations, they should really have avoided.

Among the issues that arose during this period were the genetic modification of crops, the feeding of livestock in a manner that violated their natural diet, and methods of husbandry that compromised their general well-being. It was argued that if the crops and livestock thrived, and productivity increased, there could be nothing much wrong. Others argued that stewardship of the land and its livestock should meet morally acceptable standards of decency, for which people would be prepared to pay a little more. But often it was left to the market to decide; and without good information to go on, and so many other luxuries competing for the consumer's purse, 'cheap food' tended to remain a priority.

Some of these 'progressive' practices led to disastrous consequences, as they began to spill over into animal and public health. This meant that much of our work as government vets during this period was aimed at containing the fall-out, and this preoccupied us for at least twenty years. It was a long haul, but much good work was done to remedy the damage that had been unfolding before us.

There is no doubt that biblical wisdom would have saved us from all these problems. Sooner or later, if the spiritual laws that relate to the natural world are disregarded, we can expect serious consequences. 'Clean', in biblical terms, means 'holy', or pure; 'uncleanness' means 'polluted' or 'defiled'. In Old Testament terms, cattle, sheep and goats, as cloven-hooved, cud-chewing animals, were deemed 'clean', eating only vegetable matter. This is why they were taken onto the Ark *in sevens*, and were used for sacrificial offerings to God. At the spiritual level, this foreshadowed the ultimate sacrifice of Christ as the *sinless* Lamb of God, offered in our place, so that we might be forever clean (made holy) through faith in him. Indeed, this is what is commemorated in the bread and wine of Holy Communion, so poignantly enacted at the Last Supper (Luke 22).

Some might say, 'you are what you eat'. In New Testament terms, we are in principle allowed to eat anything, provided it is *'sanctified by the word of God and prayer'*. But another saying is also true: 'cleanliness is next to godliness!'

Having therefore these promises, dearly beloved, let us cleanse ourselves from all filthiness of the flesh and spirit, perfecting holiness in the fear of God.

2 Corinthians 7:1

A WORLD OF OPPOSITES

How strange that we can live so long without even noticing that we're surrounded by a world of opposites! Light and dark, land and sea, good and evil, love and hate, male and female, life and death: so many things that affect our whole existence.

There are lots more 'opposites': can you can think of any? Right and wrong, justice and injustice, hope and despair, truth and lies, war and peace, heaven and hell. Some 'opposites' simply describe differences: for example, black and white; in other cases, they're two parts of a whole; whilst in others, they're directly against each other and could never exist together.

We see this mirrored in the natural world, both in the creatures themselves, right down to the stuff they're made of. For example, there are friendly animals and not-so-friendly ones: I'd rather own a cow or a cat, than a snake or a crocodile, wouldn't you? That's not to say that all of them don't have their place in the great scheme of things. Likewise, there are plant-eaters, and meat-eaters, and some in-between which eat anything! We might not like to watch a hawk swoop on its prey, but in the present way of things, we all have to admit there's a balance to be kept. And then there are the 'creepy crawlies', the microscopic germs of various kinds, and plants like nettles and thorns, as well as those that are poisonous. So we see good and ill everywhere we look.

When we come down to chemistry, the same principle applies: everything has a tiny electrical charge – either *positive or negative*; if you study a magnet, there's a positive and a negative end. This applies not only to the tiny atoms that make up everything, but also to the planets, the earth itself being like a vast magnet, so that a compass needle shows *north* and *south* – another opposite. And gravity and motion keep the sun, moon and stars in their place. Even so, there's heat or cold, sun or rain, wind or calm, not to mention extremes such as storms, floods, droughts and earthquakes! All these things tell us something about the Universe we now live in, compared to what it was like when it was first created, and before it was corrupted. People say, 'How can there be a kind and loving God, when there's so much suffering?' 'We see the good, but also the bad'.

Why is it like this? Would God be just and holy if he left us without correction? We were made with 'a living soul', so we'd be cut-off forever if he hadn't found a way to rescue us from the effects of the bad things we're all so prone to think and do. Right from the beginning, he arranged for his own dear, blameless Son, Jesus Christ, to take our place when he was put to a shameful death on a cross. Amazing grace! All who put their trust in him find forgiveness and eternal life. He provided for all: yet due to pride and other things, many still refuse him. Eternity itself would not be long enough to pay the debt we owe.

'...*for better for worse, for richer for poorer, in sickness and in health, to love and to cherish, till death us do part, according to God's holy ordinance* (from the Marriage Ceremony, in the Church of England's *'Book of Common Prayer'*). These tender 'opposites' speak of faithfulness under all circumstances, just as our Risen Saviour cherishes *forever* all who put their trust in him.

This is a great mystery: but I speak concerning Christ and the church.

Ephesians 5:32

CHEMISTRY

Chemistry is all about matter: the materials which make up everything in and around us. There are ninety or so naturally occurring *elements:* substances that cannot be broken down further without splitting the atom. *Compounds* are elements that have reacted together to form 'molecules' of something else, for example, the gases hydrogen and oxygen combine to form water; sodium and chlorine to form salt; and calcium, carbon and oxygen to form chalk. Then there are *mixtures*, of which air is a good example: 78% nitrogen, 21% oxygen, 1% other gasses; and tin and copper, when smelted together, form the alloy, bronze.

The elements range from hydrogen, the lightest, to the heaviest, such as gold, platinum, lead and uranium. The properties of matter include its physical state (gases, liquids or solids, depending on temperature); and whether they are metals or non-metals. Metals are usually shiny, conduct electricity, and react with non-metals in the form of acid compounds to form salts: these are often crystalline and many are water-soluble. Some metals have special properties: iron is magnetic; mercury is a liquid at normal temperatures; aluminium and titanium are light and strong; chromium and gold are corrosion-resistant. The metals sodium, potassium and calcium don't occur naturally as the pure element, as they're so reactive with oxygen. Radium, uranium and plutonium are unstable, their atoms shedding sub-atomic particles, and hence they are radio-active.

Non-metals may be gases, such as hydrogen, oxygen, nitrogen, or chlorine (chlorine and other halogen compounds, such as fluorine, bromine and iodine make good disinfectants). The most important solid-state non-metals are carbon, phosphorus, and sulphur, which together with water and nitrogen, form hugely complex 'organic' (biochemical) molecules, the basis of all living things. Energy cycles in plants and animals are based on carbon and oxygen, whilst nitrogen combined with carbon and water forms amino acids and proteins, the building blocks of life, including the genetic codes in the form of DNA. Silicon has both metallic and non-metallic features, and its compounds form the rocks. These break down to form sand, silts and clays, the basis of soils, from which we also make glass, pottery and bricks. Plant and animal residues recycled by bacteria and fungi fertilize these soils and bring them to life.

Within the above framework are some amazing details, without which the living world as we know it could not exist. Water occurs as ice, liquid, steam, and also vapour, from which the clouds are formed; it is heaviest at 4 degrees Celsius, which means the seas and rivers may ice over, but the creatures that live below the ice are safe! Oxygen in the upper atmosphere forms into ozone, a gaseous compound of three oxygen atoms, which shields us from the worst effects of harmful solar radiation. The iron core of the Earth acts like a huge magnet, by which we and some of the creatures navigate.

Blood is red because of a substance called haemoglobin, a complex molecule with an iron atom at its centre. Oxygen is absorbed in our lungs, and forms a loose chemical bond with the haemoglobin, which when circulated to the tissues of the body, is released to combine with glucose, producing energy, carbon dioxide and water. Plants are green because of a very similar molecule called chlorophyll, but it has a magnesium atom at its centre, instead of iron. Energised by sunlight, chlorophyll makes sugars out of carbon dioxide and water, releasing oxygen into the air, and thus completing the energy cycle. Within all these amazing processes, there are immensely complex chemical codes and enzyme switches, governing life's every phase and function.

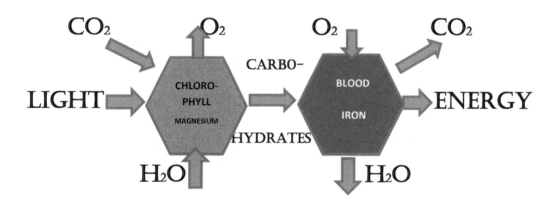

Through faith we understand that the worlds were framed by the word of God, so that things which are seen were not made of things which do appear.

Hebrews 11:3

LIFE'S CODE-BREAKERS

At school in the mid-1950's, we learned about the experiments of Gregor Mendel, a nineteenth-century Austrian monk. His work challenged earlier ideas of creatures inheriting traits acquired from adapting to their environment. He found that peas with one particular trait, when crossed with peas showing a different version of that trait, produced offspring showing one or the other, rather than a blend of each: three-quarters showed one trait, and a quarter the other. He concluded that inheritance was governed by paired entities within the cells of each parent, which he called 'genes'. At its simplest, one variant of the gene was 'dominant' and the other 'recessive', meaning that on average, a quarter of the offspring would have two dominant genes, half would have one of each, and the other quarter would be double-recessive. Therefore, three quarters would show the dominant trait, and only a quarter the recessive trait.

At the turn of the 20th century, the above discoveries began to be understood at the microscopic level, in terms of what happens when cells divide, and what happens in the male and female cells which go to make up a seed. Long filaments in the nucleus of each cell were observed to divide along their lengths, and it was understood that these 'chromosomes', as they were called, carried many thousands of genes, so that a half-copy from each parent would make up a whole, when joined together to form a seed.

It was not until 1953 that the biochemical basis of these observations was understood: almost too new for us schoolboys to bother our heads about! However, the discovery was momentous, showing how simple chemical sequences along the length of a double spiral of a substance called DNA, formed the framework for the genes that governed the code for all living things. These codes, in the form of sequences of just 4 different 'chemical letters' (nucleotides) along the strands of DNA, acted as keys for activating all the complex body processes for each individual creature, as well as governing the minor differences within each kind. Moreover, breakages or disruptions in the code, when not naturally repaired, were virtually always lethal, as when a component in an engine breaks. Such mutations are invariably harmful, and not creative.

Gradually, the complete genetic code for man and many other creatures was mapped. At first it was thought that less than 2% of the DNA was functional, the rest being dubbed 'junk': the leftovers of an imagined 'evolutionary' past. It was also said that the genome of humans and chimps was 98% the same, although less often was it admitted that 75% of our genes are mirrored in tiny nematode worms! It's hardly surprising, of course, that similarities in design and metabolism are reflected at the genetic level.

Around year 2000, a further breakthrough was made, when it was discovered that the 'junk' DNA, now called the 'epigenome', comprises a vastly complex system of chemical switches, affecting gene expression at many levels. Another, separate, set of genes is held within cell components called mitochondria, and these also affect inheritance, although through the female line only. It's now becoming clear just how everything is so incredibly and wonderfully made! Also, that within the broad limits of natural variation governed by myriads of genes and their 'switches', everything reproduces after its kind.

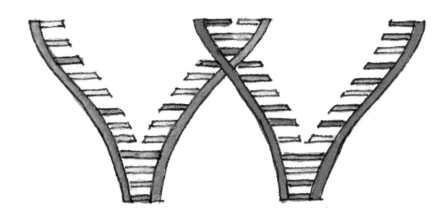

In the beginning was the Word, and the Word was with God, and the Word was God. The same was in the beginning with God. All things were made by him; and without him was not any thing made that was made. In him was life; and the life was the light of men. And the light shineth in darkness; and the darkness comprehended it not.
And the Word was made flesh, and dwelt among us, (and we beheld his glory, the glory as of the only begotten of the Father,) full of grace and truth.
And he is before all things, and by him all things consist.

John 1:1-5, 14; Colossians 1:17

WHAT'S IN A SEED?

How basic an entity of life is a seed. Often tiny, it has within it the means of growing into something beautiful and unique. What a great joy it is to see new life come forth from the sowing of a seed!

All living things start with a seed, each with a complex chemical code, which blends and reproduces every detail of its kind. How remarkable, that with all the pollen in the air, the egg or ovum within the flower of a plant will only accept the pollen of its own kind. The fertilization that then takes place brings the image of the male and female together to make the embryo, or seed, into a new individual.

Hybrids are the result of cross-breeding different varieties or breeds of plants or animals, to produce a larger or more vigorous offspring. But when plants or animals of similar species are bred together, a different sort of hybrid may be produced: for example, a mule is the sterile hybrid of a donkey and a horse.

Although scientific investigation at the microscopic level has enabled us to understand, in wondrous detail, how the male and female of the same created kind combine to form a seed, there's still great mystery attached to the subject. Even at the cellular level, in the simplest of organisms, the processes involved are vastly complex, and simply could not have arisen by chance. The subject of reproduction within God's Creation, at both the material and spiritual level, begins in Genesis, the first book of the Bible. Let none despise those divinely inspired opening chapters of wisdom and insight, upon which all the rest of Scripture stands!

Here we read of the Seed of the woman, a lineage of grace that would prevail throughout the generations against all odds, culminating in the birth of the Jewish Messiah. The genealogies of Matthew and Luke each tell their story from different angles. They show that, as promised, Messiah was indeed descended from David, but through his son Nathan, down the maternal line to Mary (Hebrew: Miriam). Joseph's line, also from David, but via the disqualified line of Jeconiah (Jeremiah 22:28-30), meant that he could only be the legal, adoptive father of Jesus (although he and Mary later had children of their own: Mark 6:3). Thus, the Holy Seed that had been promised after the Fall some 4,000 years before, was born to a virgin as God's only begotten Son, fully man, and fully God! When we consider the woeful frailty of the human side of that lineage, including gentile women like Tamar, Rahab and Ruth, we see what a miracle of grace Christ's Incarnation was. We should also note that Luke's genealogy of Christ goes right back to Adam.

The name 'Jesus' (Hebrew 'Yeshua') means 'Saviour', and in John's Gospel we read that whoever receives him, is 'born of God'. That Seed of the Divine Nature which, though it be 'treasure in an earthen vessel', will never die, but bring forth fruit to everlasting life. Death had come through the disobedience of the first Adam; eternal life had now come through God's own Son, born among us as 'the Second Adam', our great Advocate and High Priest.

Verily, verily, I say unto you, Except a corn of wheat fall into the ground and die, it abideth alone: but if it die, it bringeth forth much fruit.

John 12:24

CROSS COUNTRY BOTANY

During my teens at a boys-only grammar school in the Thames Valley, we had to do 'games' on Wednesday afternoons, which meant we had to take part in sports or athletics. As I became more serious about my studies, I grew less interested in team sports, and opted for the joyful freedom of cross-country running. This called for the utmost endurance, especially when competing against school teams up in the Chiltern Hills, where the steep, muddy slopes made the going extremely tough for us lowlanders. This physical and mental testing led to a lifelong attitude that stood us in good stead, and looking back now, I can see the wisdom underlying so many school traditions. A good education system should value and develop all children, whatever their aptitudes. Such practical love, rooted in the Christian faith, is what brings out the best in all societies.

In choosing cross-country running, I had an ulterior motive. Being out in the fields and by-ways during solo training-runs, meant I could find all sorts of interesting specimens to take back to the biology lab for study. Finding an unusual plant, one could use a fascinating book called a 'Flora', which asked a series of key questions to identify the plant's family, genus and species. You could read all about its properties, including where it grew in the world, its uses in food production or medicine, or whether it was poisonous to man or animals.

The study of a plant's cellular structure was also fascinating. It involved cutting razor-thin cross-sections of stems or other parts, and then staining them in special brightly-coloured dyes. Under the microscope, a whole new colourful world was discovered, with the most wonderful patterns of different cell-types. The stem would consist of inner bands of cells designed for conducting water and minerals from the roots, upwards to the leaves and fruits. There were usually also woody tissues, to give the plant strength to stand in all weathers. Some relied on other plants, by being of a climbing habit such as runner-beans, which we grow up tall sticks. The outer layers of stems consisted of cells that conduct the sugary sap from the leaves downwards, to nourish every living part of the plant, and to store food. Sometimes, the roots were the storage larders, as in the case of potatoes. What a blessing such plants are to man – crisps, chips and roast potatoes, for instance!

Botany opened-up a whole new world of wonder. What amazing living things plants are, with their incredible diversity, and the way they each grow best in particular environments or types of soil. You wouldn't grow water-lilies in a desert, would you, nor a cactus in a pond? And have you ever wondered how plants know how to send their roots downwards, and their stems upwards, or to twine around a pole in one direction only? Or have you considered their huge variety of shapes and sizes, flowers and fruits, to suit every environment on planet earth? Or their collaboration with the insect world, especially the bees, to achieve pollination? Quite wonderful!

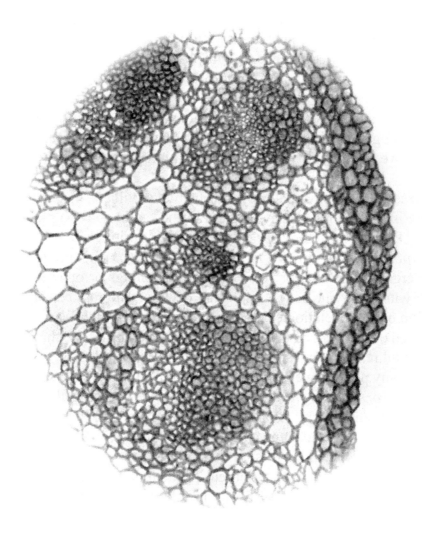

And God said, Let the earth bring forth grass, the herb yielding seed, and the fruit tree yielding fruit after his kind, whose seed is in itself, upon the earth: and it was so.

Genesis 1:11

WISDOM FROM THE COUNTRYSIDE

I've been privileged to work in beautiful, unspoilt parts of the English countryside most of my life. Here, there's a strong farming tradition, in which the skills and resources of generations are shared and encouraged. As with so many things in our culture nowadays, such a heritage is under threat, but to the discerning eye there are vestiges of nobler foundations.

I'm not glorifying all that's in the past, but am thankful for that silver and crimson thread that runs through our history. Redemptive mercy was always paid for in righteous blood, and today, we are certainly using up the capital put away for us by our faithful forebears.

It always amazes me that in every sleepy little hamlet or village, there's usually a chapel, even where there isn't a church. Many of them in these parts have a plaque announcing their identity as 'Primitive Methodist': presumably, 'primitive' in the sense of getting back to *'the faith once delivered unto the saints'* as Jude v.3 puts it. However, so many have become overgrown, derelict or converted into dwellings or other uses. This woeful sight is an open witness to our nation's spiritual decline. The real reason for this falling away is a rejection of the revelation of the Bible, something which Wesley, the founder of Methodism, warned of. Only a great Holy Ghost revival can bring the chapels to life again, for which the faithful remnant can still earnestly pray, as in Elijah's day.

Despite this gloomy picture, we may take some comfort that it's a pattern seen before in history. Jesus, a *'man of sorrows and acquainted with grief'*, specifically warned of a broad way which leads to perdition, and a narrow way which leads to life. In the course of my work in the countryside, I've had some amazing encounters with such fellow-travellers.

On one occasion, I was attending a stud bull. Whilst talking to a young man working there, it became clear that we were of a kindred spirit. Upon learning that his surname was Wedgewood, and that he was of 'Potteries' origin, I joked that he might be related to Charles Darwin (Mrs Darwin was a Wedgewood). He agreed that he probably was a distant relative. I then asked him what he thought of Darwin's ideas, and without hesitation, he came out with the view that the creatures can change within set limits (as with cattle breeding) but that one major creature-type could never have changed gradually into another. I felt this humble young man had neatly summarized the 'origins' issue.

On another occasion, I was visiting a farm on a hillside, run by two brothers. Since their mother died, they'd lived alone. Inside the neat little farmhouse was an organ, and I learned they were faithful Methodists. There was a small chapel a few yards down the road where one of them played, and they were among a tiny few that still met there. As we stood out in the yard, I'd wondered how they felt about something I'd just read about the supposed evolutionary relationship between whales and cows. We agreed that you can breed creatures within their distinct kinds, as 'nature' does, to adapt them according to need. But concerning the 'amoeba-to-man' idea, one of the brother's rough-hewn exclamation will always stick in my mind: *'you can't say a mouse 'd change into an 'orse!!*

But God hath chosen the foolish things of the world to confound the wise; and God hath chosen the weak things of the world to confound the things which are mighty.

1 Corinthians 1:27

A HYMN OF WORSHIP

O worship the Lord in the beauty of holiness!
Bow down before him, his glory proclaim;
With gold of obedience, and incense of lowliness,
Kneel and adore him: the Lord is his Name!

Low at his feet lay thy burden of carefulness,
High on his heart he will bear it for thee,
Comfort thy sorrows, and answer thy prayerfulness,
Guiding thy steps as may best for thee be.

Fear not to enter his courts in the slenderness
Of the poor wealth thou wouldst reckon as thine;
Truth in its beauty, and love in its tenderness,
These are the offerings to lay on his shrine.

These, though we bring them in trembling and fearfulness,
He will accept for the Name that is dear;
Mornings of joy give for evenings of tearfulness,
Trust for our trembling and hope for our fear.

O worship the Lord in the beauty of holiness!
Bow down before him, his glory proclaim;
With gold of obedience, and incense of lowliness,
Kneel and adore him: the Lord is his Name!

John Samuel Bewley Monsell 1811-75.

Then took Mary a pound of ointment of spikenard, very costly, and anointed the feet of Jesus, and wiped his feet with her hair: and the house was filled with the odour of the ointment.

John 12:3

Let us therefore come boldly unto the throne of grace, that we may obtain mercy, and find grace to help in time of need.

Hebrews 4:16

VISITORS FROM AFAR

Immediately after my interview to join the Government Veterinary Service, whilst travelling out of London on the train, I mused to myself that perhaps I was about to become a Civil Servant. Thumbing through my pocket New Testament & Psalms, a verse jumped out at me. It said: *'Ye are bought with a price; be not ye the servants of men.'*

Among the most amazing experiences of my career was to find myself given opportunity, on two separate occasions, to minister to the persecuted underground Church in communist countries. One entailed an official visit to such a country, and another, a visit to Britain by three foreign officials.

One day – I think it was in the early 1990s – I received a telephone call from our Regional Office to ask if I could explain our work in Farm Animal Health to three agriculturalists from a faraway, closed communist country. I was to look after them for a morning, before handing them over to tour the Veterinary Investigation Laboratory in the afternoon. Such an assignment had never come my way before, nor since.

Having learned that our visitors' understanding of English was very basic, I set out to help them by compiling a list of key words I'd be using in my two-hour illustrated talk. The idea was that they'd be able to look-up the meaning of these words in their own language, ahead of our meeting. My guests highly appreciated this, and it appeared to work very well.

What no-one knew was that I had a large map mounted on a wall in a quiet room, to help me in my prayers for that land and its people. As things began to ease and the country became more open, I used to despatch an Easy-English Gospel Outreach paper to certain contacts, some of whom became pen-friends. They'd sometimes request information on technical subjects; but some were also interested in receiving a Bible, so I ordered three copies, intending to post them. But as I sensed these were likely to be confiscated upon arrival, I had kept them in-hand until I felt the time was right.

My three guests marvelled when, at the end of my talk, I was able to put up that map, and invite each of them to point out the remote and inaccessible places they'd come from. It turned out that one had come from one of the remotest places on earth! They were even more amazed, and highly delighted, when I presented them with a personal copy of the Bible in their own language. This, for me, was beyond coincidence: it was a miracle of answered prayer.

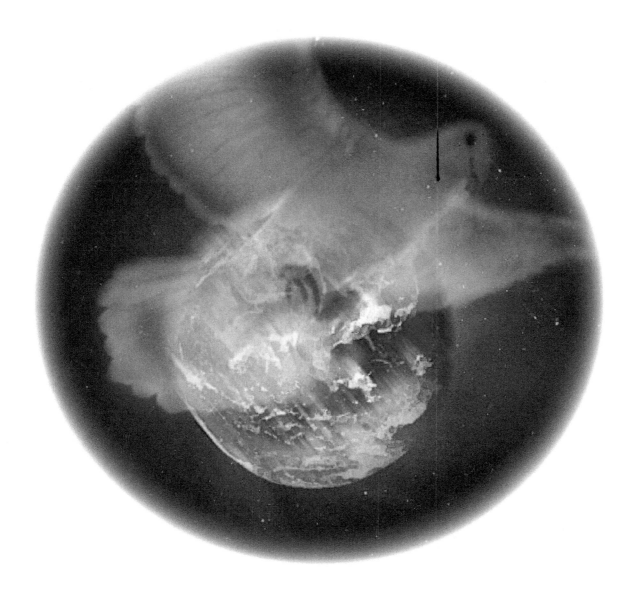

Ask of me, and I shall give thee the heathen for thine inheritance, and the uttermost parts of the earth for thy possession.

Psalm 2:8

HE MADE THE STARS ALSO

When we look up into the sky, especially on a clear evening after dusk, we see the vastness of the firmament of space, with its myriads of stars. Also, the glory of a beautiful sunset, or a magnificent skyscape of noble clouds, brings a sense of awe, as we gaze upon the ever-changing canvass above. The mood of the elements may bring glad or sombre tidings, and with the rising of a storm, a destructive power that can touch us right where we stand.

Vets work in all weathers, because the animals in their charge are often out at grass in the fields or on the hills. When a cow is found to have died suddenly, a little smear of blood from an ear vein must be taken onto a glass slide, which is then stained with a special dye and examined microscopically for Anthrax: an acute bacterial disease which causes sudden death, and is also dangerous to humans. Its spores can live for many years in the soil, but usually come into the country in contaminated feed imports from the tropics. If positive, such carcases would have to be burned on the spot. But a recent thunderstorm, with scorch marks on the hide, would lead instead to a diagnosis of lightning strike. I once knew of five cattle found dead under a tree, after a thunderstorm the night before: no need to look for anthrax there!

The old hymn *'Rock of Ages'* is said to have been inspired during a storm, when the Reverend Toplady (1740-78) sheltered in the crevice of a large rock in the Mendip Hills. Many other hymns and stories relate to fearful storms at sea, as when the Apostle Paul suffered shipwreck as a prisoner on his way to Rome: *'And when neither sun nor stars in many days appeared, and no small tempest lay on us, all hope that we should be saved was then taken away.'* But Paul heard from God, with the result that all 276 on board were saved, landing on the island of Malta (Acts 27-28).

The sun, moon and stars govern our lives on earth in perfect mathematical harmony, there being so many attributes that favour life in all its rich and wonderful diversity. Such an awesome combination may not exist anywhere else in the Universe, and even if it did, it is surely fanciful to believe that, of itself, it could generate living things. To quote Sir Isaac Newton (1643-1727*), 'This most beautiful system of the sun, planets, and comets, could only proceed from the counsel and dominion of an intelligent Being.'*

From where we as tiny grasshoppers stand, the wonders of our solar system, and the billions of stars beyond, inspire such awe. In the words of David, the Psalmist: *'When I consider thy heavens, the work of thy fingers, the moon and the stars, which thou hast ordained; what is man, that thou art mindful of him?'* And long ago, in the time of Moses, we read of a mysterious star which would rise out of Jacob, a Sceptre out of Israel (Numbers 24:17). It led to Bethlehem, to a new-born babe, wrapped in swaddling clothes and laid in a manger. And thus it was granted to humble shepherds, as they kept watch over their flocks by night, to witness the most glorious angelic proclamation of all time:

'FEAR NOT: FOR, BEHOLD, I BRING YOU GOOD TIDINGS OF GREAT JOY, WHICH SHALL BE TO ALL PEOPLE: FOR UNTO YOU IS BORN THIS DAY IN THE CITY OF DAVID A SAVIOUR, WHICH IS CHRIST THE LORD.'

Photo by S. Littlehales, Minsterley, Shropshire

We have also a more sure word of prophecy; whereunto ye do well that ye take heed, as unto a light that shineth in a dark place, until the day dawn, and the day star arise in your hearts.

2 Peter 1:19

DIVINE MURMURATIONS

The low humming and buzzing sound of myriads of bees swarming over a clover meadow on a warm summer's day might be called a *'murmuration of bees'*. But there's another wonder of nature, known as a *'murmuration of starlings'*, usually seen in the autumn, once the nesting season is over. Although the muffled sound of thousands upon thousands of little wing beats may be heard when directly overhead, the term is used more to describe their incredible aerial displays, as they congregate before going to roost at dusk.

As if to exult with others of their kind in the sheer joy of flight, many, many thousands of them come together to produce a huge flock that twists and turns in the sky to create the most awesome patterns. How so many individual birds fly in such inspired and rapturous unison is a mystery. I have witnessed one of these displays from my garden, and it is simply breath-taking! As the evening light begins to fade, as orderly as they began, they fall out a few at a time, dropping into the trees or other roosting sites, until the whole flock, noisily chattering as if exhilarated by the experience, quietens to a hush and settles down for the night.

The inexpressible is expressed in so many glories in the creation. We take so many of these wonders for granted, or are even blind to them; yet everywhere we look, and at every level, we see this glory revealed. The prophet Isaiah wrote: *'Verily thou art a God that hidest thyself, O God of Israel, the Saviour',* and in Romans 11 we read *'how unsearchable are his judgments, and his ways past finding out!'* As foolish, fallen, unbelieving mankind, we strive in vain to explain everything, even ending-up idolizing it, when it's really the *unseen* Creator we long to worship!

As John the beloved disciple wrote: *'No man hath seen God at any time; the only begotten Son, which is in the bosom of the Father, he hath declared him.'* It is to him that this book is dedicated. May you find it in your heart to join me in giving thanks to God in a spirit of wonder, love and praise! For we, too, are created beings, made in his image, and we shall never be completely fulfilled until we each recognize, and are personally reconciled to him, through his finished work on the Cross. For *'God was in Christ, reconciling the world unto himself'*; *'and ye are complete in him'* (2 Corinthians 5:19a; Colossians 2:10a).

Photo by beloved friend, the late Pastor Andrew Robinson,
Hazel Grove Full Gospel Church, Stockport.

For the invisible things of him from the creation of the world are clearly seen, being understood by the things that are made.

Romans 1:20a

THE SWALLOW'S NEST

Many years ago, I had to attend some calves at a derelict water mill. As I recall, it was an old brick building with a slate roof, and situated over a sluice through which the waters of the river poured. The man who kept his cattle there kindly showed me inside, where a great fluted wheel was housed. At the pull of a lever, the water gushed in, and slowly, the old wheel creaked into motion: so simple, yet so efficient, despite its age!

The wheel-house was quite a small affair, and almost surrounded the great wheel itself, with little room to spare. At the point above where the water entered was a vertical brick wall, which the revolving wheel cleared by only a hand's-breadth at its narrowest point. And there, just above, was something the man delighted to show me. It was a swallow's nest!

I believe, by then, the nest had been vacated for the season, but every year the swallows would come back to this place. They'd have come from afar: from sub-Saharan Africa, all the way to this very spot. It seemed the only way to get in there was to skim along the river, swoop up into the wheel house, and then, once inside, to hover like humming birds, manoeuvring up onto the vertical wall above the wheel, within inches of its rim.

Going back to my earliest memories at the beginning of this book, what a delight it is to hear the joyful twittering of swallows in the spring, as such feats of navigation and ingenuity are accomplished year after year. Also, the humble sparrow, whose lively chattering graces the eaves and gardens around our homes. In the Psalms, we read of that special place of sanctuary they each had, in the very house of their Creator!

Yea the sparrow hath found an house, and the swallow a nest for herself, where she may lay her young, even thine altars, O LORD of hosts, my King and my God.

Psalm 84:3

EPILOGUE

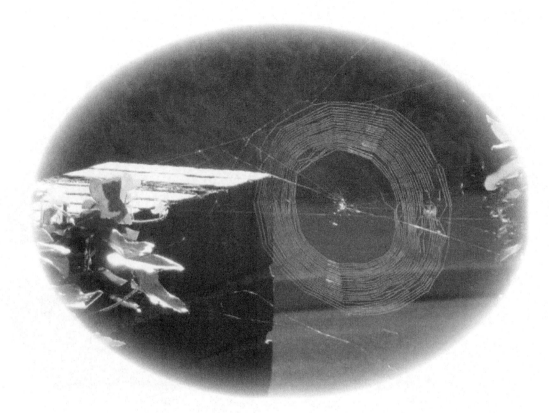

Seven Questions for The Sceptic

1. Does the 'Whole Realm of Nature' cause you to be in awe and worship?
2. Do you long for a world where righteousness dwells?
3. Have you lived a perfect life, free of all pride, guilt and shame?
4. Do you believe in absolute justice?
5. Are you ready to face the possibility of eternity in your present condition?
6. Are you willing to accept God's Son as your Advocate?
7. Could a holy God have done anything more to save you?

Then they cried unto the LORD in their trouble, and he saved them out of their distresses. He brought them out of darkness and the shadow of death, and brake their bands in sunder.

Psalm 107:13-14

God was in Christ, reconciling the world unto himself.

2 Corinthians 5:19a

And Jesus came and spake unto them, saying, All power is given unto me in heaven and in earth.

Matthew 28:18

But I said unto you, That ye also have seen me, and believe not. All that the Father giveth me shall come to me; and him that cometh to me I will in no wise cast out. For I came down from heaven, not to do mine own will, but the will of him that sent me.

John 6:36-37

The Son of Man is Come
to Seek and to Save
that which is Lost

For God so loved the world,
that he gave his only begotten Son,
that whosoever believeth in him
should not perish,
but have everlasting life.

For God sent not his Son
into the world
to condemn the world;
but that the world through him
might be saved.

He that believeth on him
is not condemned:
but he that believeth not
is condemned already,
because he hath not believed
in the name of the only begotten
Son of God.

John 3:16-18

Likewise, I say unto you, there is joy in the presence of the angels of God over one sinner that repenteth.

Luke 15:10

From Childhood To Manhood

Jesus said, *'Except ye be converted, and become as little children, ye shall not enter into the kingdom of heaven'* (Matthew 18:3), adding: *'Take heed that ye despise not one of these little ones; for I say unto you, That in heaven their angels do always behold the face of my Father which is in heaven'* (Matthew 18:10b). After his resurrection, he specifically charged Peter with the instruction, *'Feed my lambs'*, as well as, *'Feed my sheep'* (John 21:15-17). Should any stray afar and cry for help, the Chief Shepherd himself hears, and in mercy will leave the ninety-nine others, to seek and to save the one which is lost. I know this is true because, at the age of thirty, it happened to me!

In the anointed words of the Apostle Paul: *'...if thou shalt confess with thy mouth the Lord Jesus, and shalt believe in thine heart that God hath raised him from the dead, thou shalt be saved. For with the heart man believeth unto righteousness; and with the mouth confession is made unto salvation. For the scripture saith, Whosoever believeth on him shall not be ashamed'* (Romans 10:9-11).

'...till we all come in the unity of the faith, and of the knowledge of the Son of God, unto a perfect man, unto the measure of the stature of the fulness of Christ: that we henceforth be no more children....'

Ephesians 4:13-14a

128

Wherefore laying aside all malice, and all guile, and hypocrisies, and envies, and all evil speakings, as newborn babes, desire the sincere milk of the word, that ye may grow thereby: if so be ye have tasted that the Lord is gracious.

1 Peter 2:1-3

He Loves Them All

Whole Realm of Nature, boundless and diverse,
Unique and prodigious, yet blighted by the curse!
In all your wondrous beauty, marred by sin and death:
The bitter-sweet fruit, along with every breath.

Solomon-the-Wise plumbed your depths in vain,
Till One appeared, by Law-of-Love, to reign.
Entering Adam's plight, through lowly cattle stall,
He became the Slain-Lamb, to cancel out the Fall!

The lilies of the field, and the fowls of the air;
The lions and the ravens, are all in his care.
The hinds in the wood, or the flocks in the stall,
The love of his Father, he avowed for them all.

Obedient unto death, winning victory over loss,
For the joy set before him, enduring the cross!
Renewed sons of Adam, await the new dawn:
Nature's-night soon over, and in Christ all reborn!

Travailing, groaning, *Whole-Realm-of-Nature-Mine,*
Patiently awaiting, the sons of God to shine.
For God wills-not, any soul of Man to perish,
But that all should repent, the blessed hope to cherish.

And every creature which is in heaven, and on the earth, and under the earth, and such as are in the sea, and all that are in them, heard I saying, Blessing, and honour, and glory, and power, be unto him that sitteth upon the throne, and unto the Lamb for ever and ever.

Revelation 5:13

HOPE OF GLORY

For I reckon that the sufferings of this present time
are not worthy to be compared with the glory
which shall be revealed in us.
For the earnest expectation of the creature waiteth
for the manifestation of the sons of God.

For the creature was made subject to vanity, not willingly,
but by reason of him who hath subjected the same in hope,
because the creature itself also shall be delivered
from the bondage of corruption
into the glorious liberty
of the children of God.

For we know that the whole creation groaneth
and travaileth in pain together until now.
And not only they, but ourselves also,
which have the firstfruits of the Spirit,
even we ourselves groan within ourselves,
waiting for the adoption, to wit,
the redemption of our body.

For we are saved by hope:
but hope that is seen is not hope:
for what a man seeth, why doth he yet hope for?
But if we hope for that we see not,
then do we with patience wait for it.

Romans 8:18-25

PSALM 98

O sing unto the Lord a new song; for he hath done marvellous things:
his right hand, and his holy arm, hath gotten him the victory.
The Lord hath made known his salvation: his righteousness hath he openly shewed in
the sight of the heathen.
He hath remembered his mercy and his truth toward the house of Israel:
all the ends of the earth have seen the salvation of our God.

Make a joyful noise unto the Lord, all the earth: make a loud noise, and rejoice,
and sing praise.
Sing unto the Lord with the harp; with the harp, and the voice of a psalm.
With trumpets and sound of cornet make a joyful noise before the Lord, the King.
Let the sea roar, and the fulness thereof; the world, and they that dwell therein.
Let the floods clap their hands: let the hills be joyful together before the Lord;
for he cometh to judge the earth: with righteousness shall he judge the world,
and the people with equity.

Lightning Source UK Ltd.
Milton Keynes UK
UKOW07f1653300617

304425UK00006B/44/P